PROSE

...stuff I never told you...

LINDA RUTH BROOKS

GUM TREE
press

NATIONAL
LIBRARY OF AUSTRALIA

A catalogue record for this book is available from the National Library of Australia

Fiction/social issues/contemporary romance

ISBN: 978-0-6482869-8-1
9798826559772,
Cover, text design and typesetting & interior design by Linda Ruth Brooks

Prose: stuff I never told you and other books by Linda Brooks, may be purchased through online bookstores and retail outlets.

Ficus pinmula – creeping fig
(Vigilante tenant)

Contents

Ficus pimula - creeping fig

Nurses Reunion..1

Commies, feminism and ignorance...2

A day in a nurse's life...4

All about Robyn..8

The hidden boyfriend.. 14

A small lesson.. 15

Mabel... 17

Murderer.. 18

Ancient grief... 20

Maid 22

The march of feminism.. 24

Shame on ewe!.. 27

The unquiet carriage.. 31

A different point of view.. 32

Social Experiment... 35

The psychology of the family photograph................................... 38

Whatit Really Means to Be a Grownup: 39

Rundle Mall

The Adelaide chapters.. 41

A very bad day.. 42

'Refugee' from NSW 44

Expiation.. 46

A stranger stranger.. 49

Second-hand, side-by-side refrigerator 52

Vigilante Tenant Wreaks Havoc... 53

Vigilante Tenant – Part II 54

'Twas the night before Christmas... 56

India? How long? 60

Lily pilly

Avant 62

Home 64

A hungry childhood 72

Tiptoe while shouting 75

A launch pad and a ragged purse 79

I can't find my son! 82

An 'aha' moment 85

A man called Ray 87

Pedant 89

Tristan 91

Courthouse blues 93

Social Distancing Please!! 96

Doctor's office reception room 98

Ingredients for disaster 100

Terracotta glory

The great-uncles 103

Daniel 106

Roof sealer 109

The Tradesmen Wars 111

Three billy goats gruff 116

November lilies

Uncle Artie 120

It's not about the pudding 121

Mum's get-rich-slow schemes 123

You're useless! 126

The love of a mother 128

Mother's Day – Unsentimentally yours, ...129

Author 131

Nurses Reunion

We were young. And we were free. And busy, so busy. We rushed between confusion and exhaustion, elation and pride. Leaning on each other as we touched the lives of those clinging to life, or letting go. Hurtling from our naïve pasts. Falling asleep, prodded awake. Tripping and trembling, getting it wrong. And making it right.

We were young. And we were free. We laughed 'til we cried. We played, pranked and teased. Breaking the monotony—of eyestrain over the desperate fury of late night study; and brainlag over formulae and pharmacology. As we mended the broken we cracked open our own hearts. Learning to love, and to love beyond borders and boundaries. Beyond ourselves.

We were young. And we were free. We lit the flame of cellophane torches that flickered and bobbed. Down that dark corridor to our futures, in the hushed silence of the pride of family and friends. To victory. Matching tentative steps to the one in front, guiding the one behind. Could all that followed ever surpass the wonder of that night?

But how little we knew ... many times we stood side by side, posing for posterity, for camaraderie. Hand in hand, smile to smile. But who thought? who knew? ... after all this time—I would know you, and you would know me.

Who would ever have dreamed that by sharing our truth—those tales of our lives, simply told, we would find each other anew ... perhaps for the first time.

Now standing heart to heart. Truth to truth, soul to soul. Graduating once again.

Commies, feminism and ignorance

1973 was a great year to be leaving home and heading off into the world. Australia was withdrawing our troops from Vietnam. This made monumental sense to me even at the ignorant age of 17, not because I was full of political savvy, but because my brother had been drafted. His number had come up. He had been able to defer until he finished his apprenticeship, but then his 'Nasho' service was imminent. Only had a short time when he was saved by the election of Gough Whitlam and the Labor party.

I had been stiff with anxiety about my brother going to war as he appeared to have none of the qualities that would make him of any use in any army. He was shy and gentle and although he enjoyed using the 22 shotgun to shoot aluminium cans off the back fence, I had grave doubts about his enthusiasm or commitment for shooting people. Besides mum could never get him out of bed in the morning, and if *my mother* couldn't get someone up and going there was no Corporal or Sergeant on earth who could.

Don't even mention the option of becoming a medic, because when a complete stranger fell off the back of his friend's motorcycle outside our house and was quite hearty but had his face covered in blood, it wasn't the victim needing to lie down and have a drink of water but my brother. The victim sat calmly in the middle of our lounge room enjoying the attention of all and talking ninety to the dozen.

I experienced an initial period of fear and dread about the election of the Labor party because my mother had expostulated that "the end of the world was around the corner because we now had an atheist Commie government and would soon fall into Godless anarchy, forcing God to intervene Himself." When nothing remotely fatalistic appeared on the world horizon and no-one was even struck by lightning, I calmed down, thinking perhaps she had it wrong and began to relax.

When I overheard my mother calling Gough Whitlam a stupid man because of his quick wit, I developed a great fondness for him as I had also suffered at her hands for 'smart aleck remarks'. Later I went even further and decided that he was obviously a man of superior intelligence when my mother watched him on television, decrying loudly that 'sarcasm is the lowest form of wit'. She was fond of conversing with the television, perhaps with the vain hope that the person she was addressing would hear her and wither into silence. This character denunciation had often been thrown at both my father and I, so Gough's position in our affection was assured.

Equality had arrived for women. The government had just given women equal pay. I was thrilled to find out about feminism and the new freedoms for women until I discovered that it bore little difference to my mother's own philosophy of 'no man is going to damn well tell me what to do, or when to do it'. She had worked as long as I could remember as manager of the corner grocery store.

She constantly expressed amazement at the women of her acquaintance who gave up all vestiges of independence, allowed men to 'rule the roost', went without cars and driver's licenses and generally would usually take "a blind bit of notice of anything just because it came from a man."

Her pithy 'what would they know', had more effect on me than the most compelling lecture on Modern Feminism. As my father was relied upon and greatly respected by her in all matters where he was superior, I wondered what all the fuss was about. Equality of the sexes had been effectively functioning in our house as long as I could remember.

I can remember a social gathering of some of my aunts and several other women from our church. One elegant Stepford wannabee folded her daintily gloved hands and declared, "I rely on my husband for everything, I don't even know how to use the washing machine."

My mother was thoroughly stunned by this remark and regarded the woman with a look that she normally reserved for the criminally insane.

"How's that going to work for you after he's dead, Elaine?" said my mother, who would never be sent on a diplomatic mission to any country, other than one where war was considered necessary and immediate.

A tense silence filled the room. The woman blanched at the introduction of such remarks over afternoon tea and clattered her cup to the saucer, suddenly finding something of interest to focus on out of the window.

"They do you know, die I mean," added my mother emphatically, never knowing when to leave well enough alone. "Might as well face facts." My mother felt that it was her Christian duty to prepare this woman for reality, but the poor soul gave every appearance of being scarred for life.

A day in a nurse's life...

'But ... but ... the doctor said she had three weeks,' I said, clenching and unclenching my hands. I had returned to the ward to find that Mrs Partridge had died on my days off.

'At best, they're only ever guessing about how long anyone has,' said Jean, the ward nurse, touching my arm gently. She came around the nurses' station and put her arm around me. I'd only been training for a few weeks and become fond of Jessie Partridge who suffered from liver cancer. 'She looked quite beautiful, you know. We did her face and hair, then put a single red rose in her hands.'

My inner eye could not bring the vision of beauty to my memory of Jessie, with her yellowed eyes, grey skin and swollen belly.

I swallowed back tears.

'It gets easier,' said Jean. 'You can go and see her in the morgue if you like.'

I shook my head. She was gone. From this world; from me and my words of comfort and hope – the reach of my straining heart. Did she take any of my words with her? Or had they been gentling sounds like the laps of ocean on seashore. Did she hear my last words, 'I'll see you in the morning'?

Shaking these thoughts from my mind, I asked Jean what she wanted next.

'Why don't you and Cathy read to Mrs Stanford? There's a letter for her in her room.'

'But isn't she unconscious?' I asked.

'Not fully, she fades in and out. Anyway, hearing is the last sense to go and it's important. You never know.'

Cathy and I looked fearful. We were both 'newbies' – in the same class, and good friends. We still wore 'blue bags' – the uniform of the nurse in their first three months. The shapeless pale blue shift-dresses announced our ignorance to the unsuspecting world of the hospital.

'It's really irrational to fear the most helpless patients. We tackle the belligerent with less trepidation,' I said, as we walked to Mrs Stanford's private room.

Cathy groaned. 'Don't start your philosophising now, Brooks. I don't know how you fit all that in your head. We'd better get started or we'll be here 'til midnight and I'm leaving on time today.

Come on!'

I took the letter from the bedside table and opened it. 'It's six blooming pages!' I moaned.

'Here, give me that,' said Cathy, snatching it. 'Oh well, at least the writing is neat. If we were reading your scribble I'd give up now.'

I snatched the letter back. 'I'll do it. You've cast enough aspersions on me for one day.'

'Stop with the big words already. What is it with you? If it isn't tumultuous, it's exuberant, now it's nasturtiums.'

'It's not 'nasturtiums'...'

'Oh, give it a rest and read the thing.'

The writing was an elegant, but firm cursive.

'Jeez! I bet this old bird got an A+ for writing,' I said.

'Mind your language, Brooks! Hearing is the last to go - remember?'

I glared, and began.

> 'Dear Adelaide,
> Spring has come early this year. The garden is flourishing, except of course, for my favourite pale pink Azaleas.'

'Bit flowery... sure she's not related to you, Brooks... OUCH, don't hit me!'

I continued,

> 'Mavis says it's because there has been too much rain, but what would she know, she couldn't grow weeds. John Forbes died last week. He was found in the duck pond at the end of the retirement village. Such a tragedy, with him losing his wife only six months ago. Really, they're dropping like flies around here.'

Cathy muffled a snort of laughter.

'Don't start,' I said, 'you'll set me off.'

> 'Ethel Croudace thinks he killed himself over the grief, but I told her that was rubbish. No man so full of his own self-importance would drown himself in a duck pond.'

We both choked on irrepressible mirth.

> 'People have nothing better to do around here than gossip. They've got the wrong end of the stick with this. I know for a fact that John was already stepping out with Grace McKinley of Number Six - you know the one with the Pekinese and too much makeup. Not that I'm spying, mind you, but one can't help but notice these things.'

Cathy and I broke out in a fit of giggles.

'What sort of letter is this to send to a friend in hospital?' said Cathy, between chortles. 'Has the woman no sense. What are we going to do? We're only on page one. I hope this gets better. Here, give it to me – you're making it sound hilarious.'

> 'Anyway, he was always dodgy on his pins – couldn't cross the path without veering from left to right. It's MY belief, not that my opinion matters much around here, but I think he was taking Gracie's dog, Sparkles, out for a tinkle and fell in. They never found the dog.'

This mental image started us both off again. We were now giggling uncontrollably, but appalled with ourselves. I went to look out of the window to try and compose myself.

Cathy continued.

> 'Well, of course, it had to be more than that – I know they had a mug of sherry every night – together. Not that I'm a nosy parker like some around here, but one can't help what one sees on an evening stroll around the village. Well, Gracie always did leave the blinds up. Showing off, if you ask me- she's been after every man in the village since she arrived – and not just the single ones, if you get my meaning. Of course, my Bert wasn't taken in by her – not him. Called her a trumped up piece – mutton dressed up as lamb.'

By now there were tears streaming down our faces as we held our aching stomach muscles – our sensibilities for the unconscious Mrs Stanford all but forgotten.

'Who would write this stuff to a dying woman? It would make you want to jump off a cliff,' I gurgled. Cathy handed me the letter.

'I can't read any more. You read it.'

'Well, be quiet and don't look at me if I have any chance of getting this done,' I said. 'Surely there's some good news in here somewhere.'

I cleared my throat.

> 'Sheila Davis has gone to the nursing home. She fell down the back ramp and broke her hip. I told her she should use the railing – that's what it's there for, after all. At least they had a bed in the home – Eloise Franks died in her sleep. Great way to go, I say. Gracie made a cake of herself at John's funeral. Cried over everyone and begged the administration for a police enquiry. Silly woman. When a constable actually came and talked to her, she screamed and slapped his face. Apparently he was cranky for being called out to investigate an incident on someone who was 94. Mavis Burns made things worse by asking if Gracie had ever been on the stage, but I held my tongue. It isn't seemly for a lady to run her mouth off the way Mavis does.'

'This is straight out of a Jane Austen novel,' laughed Cathy. 'It's hysterical!

I ignored this remark with great effort.

> 'Of course, Mavis is my best friend, next to you, of course, my dear. I will never hear a word against her, but she does have a tendency to put her foot in it.'

'I can't do this anymore,' I said, leaning on the wall. 'We're not even past the third page and there's been two deaths, an assault on the police, a missing dog called Sparkles, midnight liaisons. I thought the elderly lived out their lives in boredom, sleeping in front of the telly. Who knew? Well, I'm just reading the last paragraph, that's it.'

> 'Well, my dear Adelaide, I must say goodbye for the moment. I have to go to Eloise's funeral. It's at the crematorium on the other side of town, but the village is taking the bus and we're stopping at the Rose Gardens for morning tea on the way home. Of course I couldn't let Mavis go alone - she's in a walking frame now.
>
> I do hope I've cheered you up, my dear, and you are soon back among our happy little group. Your friend always, Jessie.'

'Good grief,' said Cathy, 'and I thought my life was a bitch.'

Wiping our eyes and returning the letter to its envelope we sauntered back to the desk.

'How did you get on, girls?' asked Jean. 'Did that make you feel better?'

'Yes, Nurse Jean. I feel that it put the precarious nature of life back into perspective,' said Cathy, with a remarkably straight face. Turning to me she said, 'You're not the only one who knows a few big words, Brooks.' She winked.

All about Robyn

It was as disjointed a tale as ever was told. It leaped, it jerked, with a cast of characters where a name might appear, never to find its place in the story. It was here, it was there, it was everywhere. It was the ancestor of a hundred tales, all tangled together. It was told by one, and yet told by a dozen.

There she stood, our friend Robyn, former classmate and graduand, with khaki shorts (worn all year round), hiking boots, worn everywhere but bed. She wore a pale green knit shirt with an embroidered logo 'Pathfinders'. Every shirt she owns has one. When she had arrived at the reunion she had shocked us all by saying 'I have health issues, I have worms and hives'. The joke was so droll, delivered with that flat voice we knew so well, that we missed it. And then she grinned and told us all about worm farms and beehives. And I do mean ALL. She went on to tell us that her mail had gone missing many times in her life because the letters were addressed to Robyn Pathfinder.

I shall tell you the tale although it isn't mine to tell – and to make things clearer—an insurmountable task, I will use double quotes for Robyn. (I don't expect it will help much). Most of the group were sitting around the table, the evening meal over. A few of us were in the kitchen, pretending to tidy up. Monica was actually tidying up. Someone mentioned skinny dipping. 'Oh, yes,' said Robyn, 'I've done that.'

'REALLY!' said Monica, clearly shocked to the core and forgetting the kitchen. 'You must tell' (they don't call Monica 'google-on-legs' for nothing). Monica dragged Robyn to the table and called out 'Everyone listen!' So we did. A dozen or so of us, who if we confessed, had never truly listened before.

'Well,' she began, if one could call it a beginning. 'I was at a sheep show.'

This was greeted with howls of laughter, an occurrence that continued through the tale-telling as each of us held our stomachs, slapped each other and reached for tissues as tears of laughter streamed down our faces.

Robyn's eyes lit up at our screams of hilarity, and she gave the warmth of her own laughter, rarely seen. 'But that's another story.'

'WHAT!' everyone yelled.

'Tell us what you said in the kitchen,' said Monica, her eyes glued to Robyn. 'Tell us THAT story.'

Monica had missed out on part of this story that had been going on for ages, and unlike many stories at reunions, it was becoming more interesting as time went by. Mainly due to the fact that Marilyn and Robyn had formed an unexpected alliance that resembled Laurel and Hardy.

'I was doing a Pathfinder honour in worms,' said Robyn, 'or was it bees – although it might have been gardening.'

Someone asked how she got into Pathfinders in the first place.

'A man just came and got me,' she said.

'WHAT!' said a voice in the corner.

'What sort of man?' worried Marilyn.

'A man with a red panel van.'

'Good grief!' said Marilyn, 'you have to watch men in red panel vans!'

'But there were a few of us.' Robyn leaned forward, hands on knees, as if coming closer would make things clearer.

'How many?'

'Fourteen.'

'FOURTEEN! In the red van?'

Robyn giggled, clearly amused and confused that we found the details strange.

'What sort of man has fourteen kids in a red panel van?'

'He was a turkey farmer.'

There were shrieks and howls of laughter, which became the reaction to nearly every statement thereafter.

'You mean he was a SEVENTH-DAY ADVENTIST, VEGETARIAN, TURKEY FARMER!' cried someone.

'He lived near the Big Prawn. But not the Queensland one.'

'The Big Prawn?' asked Kay, 'what state are we in?'

'KEEP UP, KAY!'

Robyn laughed and waved her hands as if that would help. It didn't. 'I was living with Mrs Stork at the time.'

'What!' cried someone, 'Where are we now?'

'Just before I came nursing.' Robyn fell about laughing herself, not entirely sure why we weren't following the thread of the story.

There was a collective 'Ahhh.' Although none of us were sure where we were, but knew there'd been a jump in the timeline.

'Now, is that stalk like Jack-and-the-beanstalk or stork like carry-the-baby-stork,' asked Marilyn, displaying a sudden and unaccountable interest in spelling.

'S.T.O.R.K. She was selloneese.' Robyn spoke slowly.

'Selling knees?' I asked, feeling I might be on the way to becoming hard of hearing.

'Ceylonese,' said Marilyn. 'KEEP UP, LINDA!'

'Well,' said Robyn, squinting in concentration. 'I was asked to leave that establishment due to unforeseen circumstances.'

'MRS STORK CHUCKED YOU OUT?!?' This from Marilyn.

'No, I was working at the bank.'

'At the bank? You worked at a bank?'

'Yes,' said Robyn. 'I cancelled 49 cheques a day.'

'That's a lot of broken dreams,' I muttered.

'That's terrible,' said Marilyn, clearly favouring the underdog.

'When did you work there?'

'A few months before Christmas.'

This was too much for Marilyn who was clearly at war with poverty and deprivation. 'That's no toys for 49 children a day,' she said. 'FOURTY NINE!'

'I thought we were talking about Pathfinders,' said Monica, who was still waiting to hear about skinny dipping.

'KEEP UP, MONICA!' said Marilyn, who appeared to be the only one in the room who was keeping up with anything.

The mention of Pathfinders shot Robyn back to the turkey farmer in the red van who lived near the Big Prawn that wasn't the Queensland one. 'We started our Pathfinder meetings in the fire station. My father was in charge of the fire station, but Mum drove the fire truck.'

'YOUR MOTHER DROVE THE FIRE TRUCK!'

Robyn seemed to think that this was a perfectly normal role for a woman in 1960 and continued. 'Well, unbeknownst to the turkey farmer his house burnt down.'

'How can anyone be unbeknownst about their house burning down?'

'He saw the smoke, but that was earlier. Anyway, back to where I was—I had to leave that job.'

'Which job?'

'The bank.'

'We're back at the bank are we?' asked Monica.

'KEEP UP, MONICA! She left the bank where she cancelled 49 cheques a day and ruined the lives of 49 families BEFORE CHRISTMAS!' said Marilyn who was displaying an astonishing ability to remember details. 'Go on, Robyn, don't listen to these tossers—you left the bank...'

'I applied for a job at a café and for the interview I had to make a milkshake but the machine was broken. I got a job anyway. With the tall girls.'

'WITH THE CALLGIRLS?' (someone else was hard of hearing).

'No,' said Robyn reasonably. 'With the tall girl.'

'You never made me a milkshake,' said Marilyn, following her theme of injustice and mistreatment by her classmates (there had been an earlier episode about someone else wearing a crown).

'She wanted to be a nurse since she was three,' continued Robyn, unfazed by our interjections.

'The tall girl?'

'No, the short one.'

'What happened about the swimming episode?' asked Monica, wondering if we'd ever get to the skinny-dipping story that started the whole thing off.

'What swimming episode?' asked Mary.

'KEEP UP MARY!'

'Well that was at the sheep show,' said Robyn, 'there were five buses.' (there had been several bus stories that I've omitted for brevity, yes brevity!)

'You get on an awful lot of buses Robyn.'

'Well, the buses got mixed up,' said Robyn.

'A bit like us,' I muttered.

'What were all the buses for?'

'Pathfinders. With Helen and Russell Shulz.'

'I remember Russell Shulz. Did he get the buses messed up?'

'No, no!'

'Sounds pretty messed up to me,' said Kay, known for her superior organisational skills.

Robyn laughed. 'Someone got sick and I went to the hospital. It was late at night. I had to get medicine, which was a bit difficult I can tell you. They weren't very cooperative. I had to explain myself SEVERAL times. And then I INSISTED. They finally gave me some Maxalon, a bottle of liquid, but they weren't pleased the patient wasn't there.'

'You didn't take them! You left them behind?'

'They were too sick to take. Anyway, on the way home I felt really queasy myself so I stopped and had some Maxalon myself.'

'You took some yourself! Was there any left for the patient?'

'Oh yes, but when I got back to camp they felt much better. And that bottle lasted the whole trip.'

'Did you use it again?' asked Julianne, who manages a team and cares about protocol—but only what's strictly necessary.

'No,' said Robyn.

'No wonder it lasted.'—Joy's dry humour never fails to entertain.

'Where was Russell Shulz?' someone asked. The question of 'where was Russell Shulz' was repeated often as we tried to work out why he'd appeared in the story at all.

'The boys were inside the establishment, because of the sickness, and the rest of us were on the verandah.'

'Because of the germs.' Julianne nodded sagely, obviously proud of her infection control record.

Robyn rubbed her chin theatrically. 'So I thought - hmmm...' She tapped her forehead. 'It's a dark night - we're all tired - hot springs - the buses are mixed up - our clothes are missing...'

'Is this the 'swimming' bit?' asked Monica, clearly excited about having her earlier question answered (4 hours had passed).

'We went in the hot springs.'

'NAKED?!' everyone yelled.

'Who was with you?'

'Just Helen. Yeah, and some others.'

'WHO?'

'Couldn't tell in the dark. But there were none of THE OPPOSITE GENDER.'

'What happened to the Pathfinder meetings in the fire station with the turkey farmer who had the red panel van and lived near the Big Prawn but not the Queensland one?' asked Marilyn, who should have been a court reporter.

With face aglow, Robyn talked of badges and honours, of camping and gardening, of sashes and toggles, of adventures and camporees.

'You really love Pathfinders, don't you Rob,' someone said.

'Oh yes!' she sighed. 'Someone once asked me to give it up and I said it was like asking me to stop breathing.'

She told us she was twelve when it all began, this love for Pathfinders. Standing on a dusty road, waiting to be taken in the red panel van. A brother, a sister tagging along. Parents who worked every daylight hour God gave, every day of the week. A lonely child staring into the distance, straining to see the swirl of dust billow behind the van, heralding its arrival.

Thinking of the next learning, the next badge - for bees, for worms, for First Aid, for everything. Four sashes of honour, of memories—a life beyond the ordinary, beyond the cares of home. A life that was, for the rest of us, a phase, a giggle. But not for Robyn. It was a life that saved her.

When she had finished all those interwoven tales, however many there were, we were all in awe. Warmed by her generosity, her humility - her grace towards a bunch of self-absorbed kids fresh out of school who'd never really listened, or known her as she tirelessly worked on the fringes. She glowed as we hugged, kissed and thanked her. She'd never been a hugger but she welcomed every embrace. Perhaps she'd been a hugger after all.

She was up at dawn, packing her four wheel drive, offering us all fruit, preserves and delights as if we'd always been the friends she longed for, enjoying the overdue gratitude and praise given through new eyes.

She stood before me. 'I just want to...'

'Leave the world a better place than you found it?' I asked.

'YES!' she said, punching the air.

As I watched her walk away, I thought, you already have. Robyn Pathfinder.

The hidden boyfriend

There are so many real-life nursing situations that you will never see on RPA, or ER.

When I was doing my training, I only saw my boyfriend on weekends. This was hard to take for a sappy teenager, especially when weekends off duty were rare.

One weekend he came to visit me. I was on night duty. It was quiet on night duty. It was uneventful. Okay, that's a lie.

A patient had been discharged late in the day and their hired television was in the room. This was a prime opportunity for Prince Charming to be near me, and to watch the late night footy. I was reasonably sure that the night charge sister wouldn't want to inspect the empty rooms, but one never knows with sleep deprived despots. So, I gave him clear instructions. If the charge sister was on the ward I would press a button at the desk. This would set a flashing red light on the patient call system.

He was NOT to touch anything, but to make himself scarce down the fire stairs near the room. The night sister that night was particularly fierce, so I was a bit nervous.

The Sister arrived.

I pretended unprecedented busyness, scurrying around the ward as if the end of the world was nigh. I pressed the warning light, hoping my boyfriend had been listening to my instructions and had made a hasty, silent exit down the stairs.

But no. Clever Clogs boyfriend pressed the blinking red button, thinking that would turn it off. Not so, it set the call bell off instead.

The Sister was approaching that end of the ward. I held my breath. I thought I was safe because she never answered bells herself, preferring to bark orders at nurses.

I stayed at the Nurses Station wondering if stowing one's boyfriend in an empty room on the ward was an expulsion offence.

The Sister came back and said, 'What's wrong with the old woman in No 5? As soon as I went to answer the bell she jumped into the wardrobe.'

A small lesson

Nana May was the dearest soul. Loved by all the nurses. If ever we wanted a hug or a smile she had several ready. Not for her the remonstrations of the bitter or perplexed. Mind you, she suffered from dementia, but we nurses all thought that if we ever had to embrace the wandering of our minds becoming a permanent journey they didn't return from, then we would choose Nana May's particular style of confusion. She wore her clothes with style and aplomb, sadly starting with the outside layers first, so that a singlet or perhaps a brassiere would be put on last. No matter how often we rearranged this perfectly comfortable, but slightly inappropriate layering of her clothing, she would meticulously return to her room and undo what we'd done. She never wore the same sandals. Perhaps she thought that the right foot didn't need to know what the left foot was doing.

No matter how much time passing since nursing someone, you may forget their diagnosis, or method of leaving the world, but you never forget their personality. And hers was adorable. However, one diagnosis that we could not forget was that she was a 'pooper'. In all the annals of time, in all the medical journals there has never been a term that covers this condition. There was no aetiology for her bowel habits, or the 'result'. It was just that they 'went' whenever, and wherever they choose. The best medical description I can find for this is that it was like walking through a field and finding a cow pat. Except that it might be in the middle of the communal dining room, the lounge or on the short walks we gave her. She loved those walks. But no matter how much enjoyment we staff members gained from out meanderings her family were strangely reluctant to take her anywhere at all. In fact, it could be said that many a panicked look crossed their faces when they were visiting and she wanted to so such a simple thing as leave her room. And family was something she had in abundance.

I'm sure they loved her, of course, who could fail to? But they did seem a little embarrassed. Well, not only by her the trail she left in her wake, but also by her distinct aboriginality. None of the family appeared to have inherited enough of her indigenous genetics, but one could, if one were cynical, see a tendency to sweep Nana under the rug, along with her genetic heritage and endearing habits. This did not bode well. She had produced many children - several of whom were prominent

Ministers of Religion. One of those sons was particularly chagrined, nay entirely discomforted and ashamed – he was higher up the ranks.

We nurses thought a small, but nicely dispensed dose of humility might actually make him a better human being. We would not have undertaken such a monumentally doomed course except that he treated the staff as lowly servants who he sometimes gave the impression that we, and not his mother, favoured the inside-out wearing of her garments.

So, when he arrived and settle himself comfortably in the lounge chair opposite he would notice the arrangement of her clothing and sigh. Loudly. We could hear him from the other end of the long corridor. He would try and at least get her to wear matching sandals, but for all her submissive sweet ways, Nana May would not be constrained to have this deficit sorted. Telling her adult son who pronounced great words from rostrums and platforms that he was 'being silly' did not sit well with him.

Then the cavalry would arrive - but no cavalry that any self-respecting person would have summoned, not even in the direst of circumstances. I would bustle into the room with efficiency buzzing from my very pores and politely tell Mr Important Ambassador of Doctrine that it was time for Nana to have a walk - we needed her out of the room in order to 'set her room to rights'.

'We loved her so dearly and didn't want to upset her by having her witness our rearranging of her precious possessions and retrieving week-old zucchini pieces from her handbag, or to find her 'soiled' clothing that she may have placed in secret locations. We were only thinking of her. We were sure he understood. He wouldn't, couldn't wish her to be embarrassed or upset by our intrusion into her privacy. But it was necessary and he must be assured that we were eternally grateful not that he not only visited his dear, loving mother (unlike some unchristian types), he was invaluable to helping us take good care of her.'

He would sigh again. This time it could be heard in Outer Mongolia.

Later we nurses sat and discussed what we thought we could do when we got old and decrepit. Jean pronounced that she was going to pretend to have dementia, wander into all the other patients' room and eat their chocolates, work out who the Pastors were and pee on their mats. Marg said she would be obsessive compulsive and tidy everyone's rooms even if they put up a terrible stink about it. Gloria said she was personally looking forward to crying and complaining all day. Louise said she would carry her best hairdressing scissors and administer free haircuts. Rosa said she would feel compelled to check the dressing trolley and carry a bottle of Methylated Spirits to wipe it down properly – no one did that enough. I said I would 'dial a Pizza' for all the staff and patients, ride down the corridors on abandoned scooters and raid the drug cupboard - dispensing its contents with great generosity.

All the other staff declared we were already barking mad and left the morning tearoom.

Mabel

Mabel had been told she wouldn't make it to 100, so she lived to 101 to prove she could. She'd been a teacher for many, many years. Perhaps that why she watched us with sharp eyes that twinkled with mischief when she thought we weren't looking as we went about our nursing duties. Perhaps it's why she yelled, 'I'm the Queen of Sheba, and I would like a little QUIET in the palace!'

Yes, she had some dementia, a delightful sprinkling of it, some spice to her life and our days.

One of my nurses came to me with weary eyes, 'Sister, we can't get Mabel to eat her breakfast. Can you try? You can get around her.'

I went and sat in the chair by Mabel's bed. She folded her arms and stared straight ahead. 'They're trying to poison me,' she said.

'That's terrible, Mabel,' I said.

She turned to glare at me. I'd better not be amusing myself at her expense.

'It's poison,' she repeated, holding herself as erect as a 100 year old in a nursing home bed could.

'Let's see,' I said, picking up her spoon and taking a generous taste of her porridge.

'Don't eat my porridge, you peasant!' she said, grabbing the spoon.

Murderer

'What!'

Twelve voices rang out with the same word. It was handover time at the hospital and uncharacteristically the Charge Sister had requested all the staffs' presence. The nurses were shocked – collectively. Had they heard correctly? Surely the Charge hadn't said 'murder'?

'There is no need for that reaction. Yes, the new patient spent time in gaol for murder, but you are professionals. I shouldn't need to remind you of that.

'Blimey,' said Rachel, slumping in the chair. Her huge round eyes reflected a racing mind. Was everyone else imagining a Chopper Reid lookalike? she wondered.

'This patient WILL be treated like any other. I expect nothing more, nothing less,' said the Charge.

The rest of the handover passed in a blur.

'I'm doomed,' said Rachel, 'I get all the difficult patients.'

'That's a compliment, toots,' grinned Duncan.

'Pfft. It's obviously 'a compliment' that you're keen to avoid,' muttered Rachel.

Sure enough, the care roster had 'Hindmarsh' on Rachel's list. 'Told you,' said Rachel, to no-one in particular. She awaited the arrival of Patient Hindmarsh with undiluted trepidation. She'd scare herself spitless if she named the emotion fear, but fear it was.

'Nurse Beale, your patient has arrived,' announced the Charge through a crack in the Nurse Utility Room door. Rachel gulped. It was growing dark. The dim light in the corridors increased her anxiety.

A huge brute of man stood near the desk making the ward appear smaller. Rachel walked around the high nurses' station towards him. In front of him was a tiny elderly woman in a wheelchair. The woman had soft grey curls that were not the product of any hairdressing salon perm chemicals. The man was an orderly. Mrs Hindmarsh's face was gentle and peaceful. She smiled prettily at Rachel. Rachel returned the smile.

The days passed smoothly. Mrs Hindmarsh 'call me Jessie' had a temperament as sweet as her face. Rachel marvelled at the woman. There were very few lines on her face - no indication of a cold hardened killer, but kill she had. The nursing notes were scant on the subject but the fact of her crime and subsequent incarceration were clear.

As curiosity replaced fear Rachel found it harder to remain silent. For her, there was an elephant in the room. Finally, the temptation proved too much. It was an evening shift and the bustle of the day was over. Jessie was enjoying the afterglow of a warm shower and clean sheets. Rachel tried to rehearse her questions, but how did one breach the subject of homicide with delicacy? One couldn't, one blurted.

'Who did you ... kill?'

Jessie smiled. 'I wondered when you would ask. Sit on the edge of the bed, pet. You're so young, this might be a hard story to hear.'

Rachel did as she was bidden, her eyes never leaving the tiny woman in front of her.

'It was 1961. My daughter phoned me. She was distraught. She said she would come to me on the property for one last visit. My heart was in turmoil. She asked if her father was home and I said 'no, he's in the paddock fencing all day'. Her father had beaten me for years - was she angry with me? Could she never forgive me for having to live with that? Did she have questions I couldn't answer? The world had no place for women who left husbands. How could I explain the indefensible? I paced, and waited. She came, pale as a sheet, without my darling granddaughter. A divine baby, only three at the time. My precious delight ... she was at a neighbour's ... sorry, I'm getting off the point.'

'It's okay,' said Rachel, 'you don't have to...'

'My daughter told me her father had been molesting her from an early age. The same age as my granddaughter. That she didn't blame me - 'you weren't to know' she said. She didn't need lay blame - it fell like a shroud on me that day, I blamed myself. She'd hidden it from me - protected me. Me, the mother, who should have protected her... oh dear, sorry, love... hand me...' Rachel reached for a tissue to wipe away the silent tears. 'She said she could never visit again. She couldn't risk her daughter suffering in the same way. Then she left. The house seemed strangely cold. Twilight was falling. I heard my husband's heavy boots as he approached the house. I lined the rifle up on the window sill. I shot him.'

Rachel sat stunned. Her heart clenched. Confused, she felt a desire to clap her hands in applause. Her head spun with a million questions.

'But ... oh, I know the law was useless then, but... self-defence...?'

Jessie reached out a soft hand and closed it around Rachel's.

'You see, my dear, I didn't want to miss.'

Ancient grief

Her eyes are shiny-bright with unshed tears. Like hardened diamonds, unseeing but not unknowing. What she now knows she cannot share, cannot face. She sits amidst the others in the low care ward, in the place for which she has no name. She is 89, and for all those around her she is essentially alone, surrounded by people; but isolated by grief. Whether bending over the dining table or clutching her walking stick with grim determination she still manages to appear erect, although she has not been straight-of-back for many years.

Her son died a week ago. He was 71—in the eyes of many, an old man, but not to her, she who is older than him by the years of her motherhood. She measures all the years and days by her sons, now two. She rose early the day after he died, putting two curlers in her hair as she usually did. Then took them out again before going to the dining room for breakfast. As she always did. She puts her make-up on as usual, but now with trembling hand, heavier and imprecise. She walks a little slower. Stays a little longer at the table. She brushes the crumbs from her skirt with an absent gaze that glances, but never connects with her fellow residents. These little signs are the only indication of her breaking heart.

We do not know how to go to her, in this world of her devastation. She is from a generation where emotions have 'their place'. She will not allow us entrance to her grief, so we must leave her there, in the memorial of her own choosing.

Reaching out with guarded hand, she gently touches her son's face in the photograph by her bedside, when she thinks we're not watching. The tears struggle down her wrinkled cheeks. She hears a door open. She is so afraid to be seen exposed and vulnerable that she flees to the bathroom, to the shower, and the comfort of solitary grieving.

These are the routines she clings to desperately every day for two weeks. But like an autumn leaf she falls. Unable to fall into her grief, she falls in the shower. We find her naked and bleeding, broken and alone. The ambulance comes and she is stoic still.

When she returns from the hospital she is a little more stooped, a little more fragile. Then she begins to sit in the foyer where she has never sat before. When we ask her why, she focuses us with clear, direct eyes. 'I am waiting for the school bus.'

Leaving our reality, she has found her own. She has wandered to a safe place; a place still inhabited by everyone precious to her. Grieving and memories have combined in this new world. She lets us lead her. She doesn't ask to return to her room as once was her custom.

'Take me home,' she whispers.

Maid

I was once a maid in an expansive upper crust North Shore mansion. Why? you ask. Well, it was like this ... lots of nurse trainees were taking on extra jobs to 'earn a bit'. A friend had a regular gig at the local manor, one day a week. For reasons I've forgotten she had a month where she couldn't do the job. I'm not sure how I ended up taking it on, but I did. After all, one day a week for four weeks wasn't a lifetime. And if my mother's words were ringing in my ears that 'Linda should have been born with a maid', I chose to ignore them. I could do this.

I tapped a big brass knocker on a heavy wooden door and waited for The Butler. A tall austere woman of indeterminate age answered the door and introduced herself in clipped tones. This was The Lady of the Manor. Even though she wasn't the butler I felt I'd stepped into a Jane Austen novel. And like poor cousin whatshername my status as servant was immediately and imperiously conveyed to me by a sombre voice with perfect elocution and delivery. The peasant had arrived to get on with it.

The vacuuming required more exertion than a horror shift on the ward. The ancient vacuum cleaner was an upright model and proved more cumbersome to manoeuvre than a bus. Worse still, every room had not only carpet but fringed rugs of Persian origin. Rug beating is really overrated as an activity and should be included in the Olympics. These were 'frightfully expensive' and great care was needed, which was confusing while whacking a rug the size of a football field.

Then it was off to be Cinderella, albeit without the hindrance of The Ugly Step-Sisters. 'Remove ash from fireplaces'. I got lost and had to interrupt the Lady of the Manor who was ensconced at an ornate timber desk doing obscure but extremely important things. She sighed heavily. I was unsure what to call her so I resorted to 'Madam'. She sighed again. I got lost a lot and she sighed a lot. Eventually I found what I can only describe as an external, square 'hole in the wall' from where the ash had to be removed. Madam assessed my attire and expressed regret that I had not provided my own apron or overalls so I spent as long dusting myself off after I'd finished in order to be fit to re-enter the abode as I'd spent shovelling the mountain of ash.

When I'd finished she smiled. It was terrifying. This was not a face accustomed to smiling and clearly the poor soul could have done with a bit more practice before trying it out on unsuspecting members of the lower classes. She expressed pleasure at my work ethic and prepared the clothes basket and the iron in the kitchen. She left me to set it all up and waved an indifferent arm, mumbling about 'taking a few minutes break'. What I was to do with said break was unclear, but the junior master of the house soon stepped into the breach after his mother left. A tall rangy young guy about my age wandered into the kitchen and said hello. Did I want toast and jam? He was getting some for himself. A capital idea, I thought, getting into the Jane Austen spirit, but I merely responded, 'sounds great, I'm ravenous.' He prepared several thick, slices of extraordinary toast with delicious jam and set a place for me at the table. This caused me to totally revise my opinion of the upper classes. He was at Uni and we were soon knee-deep in a discussion about some fascinating philosophy when his mother returned.

Madam did not smile. She frowned. It was a severe expression that was more terrifying than any of the others. But I'd cut my eye teeth from the age of six on stern, uncompromising teachers and was amused. I was, in fact, smack in the middle of a Jane Austen novel. However, Madam was far too well-bred to screech at The Help so she focused on the offspring who had wantonly breached the rules of etiquette by mingling with the maid. 'Brayden, don't you have something better to do?' she said curtly. Brayden failed to take the hint and wandered even further into hazardous territory. 'No Mum, I've done my assignments and I was just having breakfast with Linda.' Madam's face reddened to a dangerous shade and Brayden finally realised he was in hot water. He didn't know why, but I did. He was on first name basis with a peasant. And one of the opposite gender. Brayden left to undertake some urgent chore of her speedy invention and Madam left me to get on with ironing the table linens.

After that Madam's critique of my domestic skills plummeted. I was 'rather slower than expected with the ironing'. This was followed by a 'general tizzying up of the kitchen and dining rooms', my final task for the day. When she returned, Madam had recovered her composure, remembered her highborn manners, thanked me, then reached into a tiny coin purse, removed a few notes before again attempting a smile. 'Do come again dear,' she said, with a voice aiming at warmth but veering towards desperation while taking a sideways look at the upper rooms where Brayden was locked in the tower. Good Help must have been impossible to find, and one had to accept mediocre. After all, one couldn't be feasibly expected to do things oneself.

When I didn't immediately respond, she added, 'I'm quite satisfied with your work today and will be glad of your help for the next three weekends.'

In spite of being shocked by the fact that she wanted me back, like Madam, I recovered my composure.

'That's awf'ly kind of you Madam, but I really don't feel I'm cut out for this Maid lark. Know what I mean? But thanks anyway. You've been a deah.'

I was maid for a day.

The march of feminism

I didn't need Germaine Greer.

I'm sure thousands of poor downtrodden women did. But with the indomitable Elsie Brooks as my mother – I needed no such education. Giving my father the ultimate accolade by saying–'Your father can do anything' was no prelude to submissiveness. Having her own career in an age where many women stayed at home meant that it was none of Dad's business what she did with her own bit of money.

However, I was delighted when I went to do my nurses training to find we had equal wages. We touched on feminism at 'The San' and a touch was all I needed. I said nothing on the subject because I was confusing enough to the known universe. Everyone had decided I would pursue an academic life, without ever listening to a word I said.

And after hearing a lifetime of Mum's wonderful philosophies, I had what I needed. 'Don't believe something just because it came out of the mouth of a man', 'A woman is mad if she doesn't keep her own bank account and independence', 'Why doesn't that woman get a driver's license and a car and stop whining to her husband to take her everywhere?'

The closest my parents came to arguing over money was when Mum said–'You pay a fortune for those flipping tools', and Dad replied, 'don't think I haven't seen you sneak shopping into the house when you think I'm not looking.' I joined in with 'but Mum, Dad fixes EVERYTHING with those flipping tools.'

Ever fair-minded, Mum simply said, 'That he does, and a fine job he makes of it all. He should be paid more. I have half a mind to go and tell the factory to give him a raise.'

This statement so terrified my father that the discussion ended.

Years later, I attended the University of New England to do Nursing Admin. It was 1984.

I was gobsmacked to find that half of the nursing course subjects were on feminism. Were they still banging on about that in Australia? I thought. 'Patriarchy in Nursing' was a stitch up. We registered nurses who'd worked on the job for years wondered if the lecturers had ever worked in hospitals. Only in theatre during surgery was the doctor revered, and that applied equally to the female doctors. On the wards the Sisters ruled. If a doctor failed to complete notes, it was HE who was hunted down and hauled over the coals. If his writing was illegible, he was phoned to clarify or told—'What makes you think you can scrawl like that in MY nursing notes?

We found out later that many of the lecturers weren't nurses.

The feminist lecturers found me annoying. I was petite with fluffy blonde hair - a crime of vast proportions. They found me confusing - I held strong opinions, debated and delivered addresses on behalf of my group, so they couldn't quite fit me into the ditz category. I was always with a group of guys. Never mind that there were several other women there too, the feminists still stared with disdain at me.

The guys opened doors for us, brought coffee and made sure we had seats. When we were 'studying' in the lovely pubs in town, there was always one of the guys on hand to tell any guy giving me unwelcome attention to—'Leave my wife alone.' I mentioned the reaction of the more militant feminists, in what I thought was an amusing anecdote to the guys. I wasn't prepared for their protectiveness. They were appalled. Next morning tea time they upped the ante. One carried my coffee, one carried a teaspoon, one a saucer, yet another a biscuit and the cheekiest of all - a sweet atheist who respected my beliefs, although they made little sense to him, carried my chair. They did this with great ceremony to a packed audience in a line behind me as if I was Cleopatra.

Their efforts to make a point were not wasted. The most militant feminist lecturer approached me. 'How can you respect yourself with every man in the place waiting on you hand and foot?' she said.

I didn't think she wasn't angry, just confused. The guys, however – were angry.

'She needs a good root,' said one.

I cringed. And I was fairly sure she'd heard. I told him that he had just ensured that he'd fail, not only her subject, but the entire course. He was the Director of Nursing at a major hospital with a resume that would curl anyone's toes, and I was a humble ward sister in a nursing home. After that, he wrote first one, than another stunning essay for Best Practice Nursing and she gave him abysmal marks, even though she continued to give me distinctions. He hadn't believed he'd be punished, so just to see what she'd do, I wrote an essay for him - it too received a fail.

My reply to the lecturer on that day is still my philosophy—'If I am given respect from whatever source, I feel fabulous.'

To rebel and celebrate I slid down the banister in the grand foyer. If you're ever there - do give it a try - they are superior banisters for sliding.

I topped off my time there by organising a group to climb over the huge fence around the swimming pool on a hot humid evening straight from the fires of hell. The nun in our group declined to come, but four of us scaled the walls. It was dark. Slightly naive I didn't realise one of the guys was more than a little drunk than he appeared. He fell down every terraced section followed by 'Farrk!' We had a marvellous time in the cool water. Being born on the coast I've always been addicted to water.

The lights came on in the caretaker's cottage, flooding the pool area. More colourful language erupted. The others saw their impressive careers ending with arrests and front page news. I was upset the episode was over.

I thought they would find it just as easy to exit as it was to enter. I'd been climbing things all my life. Maybe their nerves kicked in because they were making hard work of it. The inebriated guy was in his jocks. Having declared he'd come along but wouldn't get in the water, he changed his mind at my urging. He couldn't scale the fence. Maybe the alcohol in his blood had kicked in. What would I know – I had never imbibed the stuff. He was panicking so I threw his clothes over the fence.

There I was, pushing him and helping him get a toe hold on the steel fencing.

'For someone who doesn't believe in feminist crap, you sure know how to ... oh fuck! - who's got my trousers?'

Shame on ewe!

It was a balmy spring day that followed a dismal week of rain. The children were antsy in the first activities of the morning at the preschool where I was a mothercraft nurse for the children under two. We could see a long day ahead of us, dealing with bored and cranky children who'd spent the last week indoors.

So Susan, the director, decided that we would take them all for a walk. They were excited about being able to go outside. There were many quiet walks in the backstreets near the preschool - the roads soon became rural and the promise of fresh air and exercise was tantalising to the staff as well. Except for Katherine, who declared she'd rather put her head in an oven than go. She'd been to a prestigious dinner with her scientist husband the previous night.

'I drank enough red wine for three day headache,' she moaned. 'It wasn't even worth the trouble. It was still the most Godawful boring night.'

Now, Katherine was a gem. There was no task she wouldn't tackle or job too menial. Her dry wit and unique take on life entertained us daily. But someone had to be on site because we had a nursery in the preschool, and there were two babies sleeping. Gabe and I worked in the nursery. We had three toddlers who would enjoy the outdoors, so we were more than happy to let Katherine stay behind.

'Put your feet up, Katherine. The babies will sleep a bit longer,' said Gabe.

'Where?' asked Katherine dryly. We grinned. The nursery was tiny and Katherine was very tall.

Susan and Gabe knew the ropes better than I, so they did head counting and calculation of staff to child ratio. Susan declared that we were fine to go. This decision delighted everyone. The children sensed adventure. They demanded their gumboots plus a hundred other things they didn't have, along with a few things they didn't.

'Are we takin' snacks?' asked Brendon, whose life revolved around food.

Gabe moaned. Brendon wisely took that as a 'no'. He was used to being denied food. But not quite as much as he should have, because he was overweight at four.

So off we went. The children were very well behaved. That was more due to Gabe and Susan than to me. They knew about large groups of small children and motivating stragglers, whereas my single useful talent seemed to be lying on the floor getting smeared with Vegemite and paint.

This 'look' made going to the bank a bit embarrassing, but the tellers became accustomed to my appearance after a while. However, there was always another customer who gave me an incredulous look. There I was, with a business banking bag looking like a preschooler myself.

The children were having a wonderful time. We came across a paddock of sheep. I don't remember who it was, but I know it was someone other than me, decided that it would be great to wander among the sheep. I didn't have enough knowledge on mingling with sheep in their natural habitat to give an opinion, so I shut up.

The children were overjoyed. Gabe and I each had either a toddler or one of the younger preschooler in each hand. To start with.

The sheep proved to be placid and nonchalant. Except for one ewe that had 'gotten out of the wrong side of the...' well grass, I guess. She started charging the children, and she was a good aim. Not stupid either - systematically she knocked down the smallest of the children. The older children giggled to see the little ones go down like ninepins. This ewe would go well in a bowling alley.

As soon as we picked one toddler up, another went down.

'Baa!!!' we'd hear, followed by an equally loud, 'Waa!!'

This went on for a short time, which seemed like a long time. The ewe was running at what seemed the speed of light, all over the paddock. We staff ran to pick up the latest victim and comfort them. However, we couldn't pick them up as fast as the ewe could knock another one down. Which was a bit time consuming. And probably the reason we didn't seem to have a strategy for actually dealing with the sheep. Well, if any of us did, you wouldn't have known.

The whole thing was becoming very worrying. This sheep had energy to burn. She appeared to be happy to spend all day at this, while we couldn't seem to rescue the tots fast enough to even think about heading out of the paddock, and danger.

Then, the ewe ran past me. Without thinking I kicked it in the belly. It went down like a tonne of bricks. It didn't move - not even a twitch.

'Quick! Get out of the field now!!' I yelled.

No one moved. 'Run!' I yelled, thinking a shorter version would do the trick.

It didn't.

'I can't believe you did that!' said Gabe.

'What?' I said.

'What about the poor sheep?' she said. Susan was looking a little gobsmacked as well.

'Who cares about the bloody sheep?' I said.

'It might be dead,' said Gabe.

'Oh well, you stay here and administer CPR while the rest of us get the kids the hell out of here,' I muttered.

'It's probably winded,' said Gabe, still holding firmly to The Rights of Outlaw Sheep.

'You live in hope,' I said, 'anyway, that's nothing. I've been winded twice. It'll survive. I did.'

'That would be you, Linda. I daren't ask how that happened.' Gabe was smirking by now and beginning to lead the children to the gate. 'I don't know how you can NOT care about the sheep, just the same.'

'I'm a vegetarian. I'm not the one who buys carved up sheep from the butcher, and has mutton stew or lamb sandwiches. But I do care about parents asking questions because their kids have been mowed down by a deranged sheep that's twice their size.'

We arrived through the gate, and all three of us burst out laughing. Some of the children joined in – some because it was funny, and others because they thought we were funny. As we looked back the ewe was scrambling to her feet. She looked fine, if a bit dazed.

'See,' I said, practising my self-righteous look. I was beginning I deserved some praise. But I wasn't about to be granted 'hero status'.

All the way back Gabe kept repeating in a stunned voice, 'I can't believe you did that!'

I didn't have an answer. I didn't know any better than her, other than it was instinct. Which would have been fine, but it seemed it was an instinct that nobody on the face of the earth other than me would have had. I had no farm experience, but I did have an older brother who thought I was put on the earth for him to finetune his practical jokes. 'Jokes' that had no practical element at all, but incorporated all the hallmarks of The Three Stooges antics.

When we arrived back at the preschool, the babies were awake and howling. A grateful Katherine handed them over to Gabe and I, as the children gathered around her with their excited versions of the sheep incident.

'Well, that puts paid to the parents not finding out,' sighed Susan, who had all the responsibility of explaining everything that went on, and everything that didn't. Parents busy with their own lives were awfully picky about how their children spent their days at the preschool, even the ones who all the appearance of not spending five minutes with the children themselves.

Katherine howled laughing at the kids' stories. Then Gabe gave her the 'real' version of the Sheep Kicking staff member who incapacitated a hyperactive ewe. But now even Gabe was chuckling. I think.

'Oh that's priceless,' said Katherine, 'I wish I'd been there. As usual, I miss all the fun. Trust Linda. Go girlfriend!'

I glowed. I was happy to accept any praise.

As we suspected, the first thing the children wanted to tell their parents when they came to pick them up, was the story of the head-butting sheep. Unfortunately for me, the tale wasn't restricted to the ewe's activities.

After one or two of them pointed at me and said, 'There's the lady who kicked the sheep and it lied down for a sleep,' I decided to get busy inside – away from the attention.

A mother and son passed the window where I was pretending to clean. The boy saw me. He started enthusiastically telling his mother, 'You shoulda seen it, Mummy. That lady kickded the big sheep *so hard* the others thought it was dead, and they were going to call a sheep amb'lance and operate on it. The lady was as fast as Superman. Whoosh! Bang!'

I cringed and sunk out of sight.

'Thank Goodness for that,' said the mother.

I sighed with relief. Perhaps I wouldn't get arrested by the RSPCA. Or animal rights. Or lose my job.

The unquiet carriage

I gave my cousin a wistful hug goodbye, before clambering on the train. I'd had a busy few days with my cousin's family. Out and about. I must confess that I'm not good with too much Out and About. My mother was known to say that I was born tired. And this day I was very tired, and bearing with a headache that could split bricks. I was looking forward to the three hour train trip home. The gentle rocking of the train with only the rhythmic sound of the rolling tracks.

However, the carriage was packed with excited primary school children. My designated seat was in the middle of the crowd. A big competent rail warden – sorry, steward, sat me at the back with a group of young energetic teachers, who gave all the appearance of looking forward to the trip as much as the kids. They apologised to me.

'No need,' I said, 'I've been on more overnight excursions as parent helper than I can count.' I told them I was a former registered nurse and regaled them with past trip disasters. We giggled more than the kids.

One regal old dame, with a dumpling beehive hairdo demanded another carriage. 'I didn't pay for a four hour journey to be put in with CHILDREN,' she said with clear disdain. Several other old women chimed in, obviously parents of perfect children and grandchildren.

The steward put them in first class. I began to wish that I'd complained.

As the train took off for Sydney, the Taronga Zoo, and parts unknown the noise level rose. One girl smacked herself in the nose. Boys quarrelled, turned lights on, yanked on curtains, dropped food and were called one by one to sit with the teachers – not a situation many enjoyed.

One streak of grumbling rebellion named Jai was a regular.

Another cute little fellow came meekly to the teachers. 'Magnus is annoying,' he said politely.

I bit my tongue, tempted to say that was the job description for some kids.

This round-faced boy was seriously cute.

'We'll swap you with Brad, then,' said a tiny, bubbly teacher.

'Oh no!' he begged, 'then he'll just annoy my friend Reed.'

A different point of view

What would we look like to Martians? What if there was life on another planet and they observed us? This is what I think they would say.

'The Third Planet from the Sun is populated with an interesting, but strange species. They call themselves 'humans' or 'homo sapiens'. They also call themselves 'mankind' even though there are females in the species. There are many other names they give themselves, and this is very confusing. They have not perfected an effective form of communication, even though they have quite advanced equipment, because their language is always changing. To make things worse, even though they travel and interact, each landform has a different language. On closer inspection, we find they have drawn lines all over the planet and made them into different areas which they call 'countries'. The species constantly talk of being proud to be part of 'mankind', but they persist in claiming that their own 'countries' are superior to the others. This is very confusing to us.

Sometimes they invite humans from other countries to come and live in their countries, but they do not appear to be receptive to uninvited humans. Sometimes when they visit other countries they take inventions called 'weapons', and decide they wish to own that country as well as their own. These 'weapons' cause great destruction to property and the humans who live there. Sometimes when they visit with 'weapons' they say they wish to bring peace to the other humans. They call this process 'war'. This is also very confusing.

Many devastating events occur in the natural world. These are caused by weather patterns and other forces of the universe. Planet Earth appears to be particularly afflicted with these events that the humans call 'Acts of Nature' or 'National Disasters'. Although the humans appear to have intelligence and a capacity for memory - and also have written records, they seem to forget these events are always possible, because on each occasion they don't appear to be prepared. They speak with great wonder about these things as if they have never happened before. However, as soon as one of these events occurs, their memories appear to be activated and they speak of past disasters with great clarity. This is also very confusing.

The Planet Earth is a place of great beauty. It is envied by all the species in the universe. The humans do not seem aware of this, even though they have travelled to other planets. Very few humans appear to enjoy this great gift. They place great importance on constructing huge tall rectangular buildings, where they gather in large numbers and perform many repetitive tasks. Getting to these buildings involves the use of inventions they call 'transport'. Sometimes a 'transport' can convey large numbers of humans, but often the humans have only one small 'transport' called a car. Humans spend much time in all these forms of transport. This activity is not something that appears to give the humans pleasure. They become angry and frustrated. Most of them appear to have the ability to shut down their brain activity during this process. This is also very confusing.

Arriving at the large buildings, which they call their 'destination', does not seem to give them any pleasure either, even if they have travelled great distances. Much of this 'transport' process involves injury and other problems, but they appear unable to cease these activities. There are many layers to these buildings. The humans appear to pay homage to those humans who inhabit the top layer of the building. The humans in the top layer of the building reward the humans in the lower layers with what they call 'currency' or 'money'. The humans have a great love of this 'currency' and have many aspects to their worship of it. The most common form of this 'currency' is small painted sheets of paper with numbers on them. These are much sought after, and are passed around between the humans with great speed. They take these sheets to buildings and speak of 'growing it'. There appears to be a great number of human beings who take these sheets from other humans, and then call it their own.

Many of the humans involved in this activity wear very fine clothing. These humans smile a great deal. They promise the other humans that if they give them their currency sheets, they will get many more back. This doesn't happen very often, but the humans continue to follow this form of homage. Some people worship this 'currency' so much that they refuse to part with any of it. Sometimes, all the 'currency' on the planet seems to disappear, and everyone talks about this event as a 'crash'. The humans appear to suffer the same anxiety at these times as they do when they experience the 'Acts of Nature' called 'disasters'. This is very confusing.

There are occasions when the humans take breaks from the mass activity in the buildings. They engage in what they call 'holidays'. They appear to also worship the concept of 'holiday'. It is much spoken of, and with great excitement. Their voices sound different at these times. Their brain activity appears to be stimulated and they plan these events with much happiness. This process of 'holiday' becomes a migration of the species. It appears necessary to leave their own part of the planet, regardless of its beauty, to 'transport' to other areas of the Earth. They spend much 'money' for these 'transports'. This is also very confusing.

Humans spend a great deal of time in front of inventions. Most of these are square or rectangular boxes that emit light. The humans have many forms of these and this appears to be another form of worship they regard highly. However, like the activities in the large buildings there are many humans who have great resentment towards these inventions, although they continue to worship them. This is also very confusing.

Humans have very strange habits at certain times of the year. The year is appointed to have a 'beginning' and an 'end'. At the 'end' of the year all the activities of the humans increases. There is a greater interest in 'transporting', exchanging 'currency' and the activity of 'holiday'. During this time of the year the humans appear to have a greatly increased need for food, so the activity of obtaining food becomes frantic. Although their human need for sustenance remains the same, nearly all the people on the planet are involved in this frenzy.

At the same time, most of the species also become more active with 'currency'. They visit other buildings they call 'Shopping Centres'. There, they give away their sheets of 'money' in large amounts. In exchange they are given many items which they convey to their places of living, called 'homes'. They wrap these items in large colourful sheets of paper. Then the humans exchange these items with each other. They do this on the same day all over the planet. On that same day they gather in groups, which they call 'families'. Although there is great excitement among the young of the species, there appears to be little pleasure for the adult of the species. Then the day after, the humans take the items they have received back to the 'Shopping Centres' where they exchange them once again. This is also the beginning of another frenzy of exchanging 'currency' which lasts for about one lunar cycle and is referred to by the humans as 'sales'.

At the end of this cycle the human's brain activity again becomes dormant. This new time coincides with the 'beginning' of the next year. Many of them speak of 'depression' and a great sadness at the lack of their favourite item to worship – this 'currency'. This is the most confusing aspect of activity on Planet Earth.

They appear to have a great fear of other species visiting their planet. *This is extremely confusing.* Why would we want to visit a planet when the species inhabiting it appears to have no concept of running the place?'

Social Experiment

Remember the days when 'social experiment' meant reading a psychology book by Skinner, or perhaps, Jung and then asking a selection of willing people a few pertinent questions.

Now, here we are in the year of two-nought-whatever (the 'noughties') and a 'social experiment' is conducted on live television and called reality TV, which interestingly enough is the farthest situation from reality as one could possibly imagine. Take twenty or so people, interview them, pick the most opinionated and controversial, add someone who invented the word 'drama', select someone else who cries at the drop of a hat – and mix... if James Bond was placing the order it would 'shaken *and* stirred'. Give them a little power against each other, let them play musical beds, mess with the food quota, deny them access to the outside world and you have... no – not a POW camp, but 'entertainment'. And all this by people who sent in applications expressing how desperately they want to be there and aspire to willingly to honour and obey Big Brother. A significant act of conformity.

My personal summation would come under the broader category of Gross Stupidity, but what can you expect from someone with a convict heritage entailing a dash of anarchy? After all, my great great Grandfather John Handeboe was transported from Ireland for the proverbial offence of stealing a sheep. I don't think the courts had much imagination in those times because I doubt if there were enough sheep in existence to account for the number of sheep-stealing convictions that led to transportation. If we gave the problem to the politicians to 'put a spin on it' they would probably call it 'Colonisation and Relocation of Essential Services via Involuntary Emigration'.

On the night that my ancestor, Mr. John Handeboe of County Westmeath was arrested his brother James, and a cousin were also sought, but they escaped the well-armed law enforcers of 'An Garda Síochana' and sailed for North Carolina where they subsequently battled the Brits. John was not so fortunate and was hauled before the courts to face the accusation of sheep theft. The mind boggles at the thought of a sheep that required three grown men to ensure its capture. John Handeboe, 'farm manager', 'carpenter', 'cobbler' and 'fettler' filled in the necessary forms. However, he seemed to display a contrary frame of mind and had written illegibly until the bottom of the form where he added the words 'no master' of his own accord. A significant act of anarchy.

I would like to conduct my own social experiment, but first I must tell you a story... In 1987 I wanted to sell my house. I had bought it from the owner, a builder when I heard about it on The Cooranbong Grapevine. I woke one morning and before my brain had time to question my actions I'd made a hand-painted 'FOR SALE' sign and banged it at the front of my house.

'You're a right scream, Linda,' said Jimmy Pritchard, my neighbour as he chortled all the way down his long drive. 'Do it y'self Real Estate – what next?'

The house sold before nightfall.

In 1992 I had a house to sell in Drayton, a tiny community near Toowoomba, QLD. This was different – there would be no DIY. If anyone passed the house it was because they were lost. I went back to the rotund loquacious realtor who sold us the house and pronounced us 'lifelong friends'. To cut a long story short, it went like this – 'I know and live in the area – I'm your man', 'after careful consideration I believe...' 'in this prime rural location it's 'a dead cert' at $** in the current market'. I moved to NSW. 'Not a bad idea to vacate the house,' said Mr Dickens, sole proprietor of Drayton Realty – staff of one. Then the tone changed - 'there's been limited interest in the property', 'it would be in your best interest for a sale to drop the price'. The house sold for ¾ of his original 'guesstimate'. And guess it was.

Is real estate the only area with so much guesswork? A surgeon doesn't up his price because of a downturn in the scalpel market. A builder or tradesman works out a quote and you sign a contract for a fixed price.

However, I can't help but ask the question that if the realtor 'has his finger on the pulse' and names a price – one that often decides whether or not a vendor can afford to sell, why then after only a short period of time, when there has been no Wall Street Crash or mass suicide of financiers from tall buildings, why does the price fall at least $15,000 in a fortnight?

There's only one conclusion. One of the estimates was wrong. Or. It's really a great big game of 'bluff and tell' where you're expected to believe each new 'reality' as it's presented, along with the jargonised spiel that defends their latest *latest* carefully calculated position. It's always an interesting twist when the very person who priced the house has been overheard saying, 'They were asking too much.' *Really!*

In my most recent attempt to sell my current home, with one of the realtors, the whole thing reminded me of being on a seesaw with the school bully.

My house devalued faster than pork in a synagogue. In my intended new place of residence I was asked if I was going to put a deposit down to show my intentions even though my questions weren't answered. It went thus.

'The patio at the back has a slope,' I said.

'No, it doesn't.'

'If you had a meal out there it would be 'Fawlty Towers',' I said.

'It's flat.'

I began to feel like Galileo.

'Then there's the orange stain down the bathroom wall,' I said.

'I thought you said you could paint?'

'I'm not inclined to paint walls until I know if orange strips indicates rusty pipes and thus entire new plumbing. And about the cleaning...' I said.

'That's been done thoroughly.'

'I guess that explains the spoons still in the drawer then,' I said.

I received a well-rehearsed look that was also reminiscent of my schooldays. In my mind I could see both ends of the seesaw collapsing. I was left with an untenable situation. Hurt and confused I pulled out.

Why do we feel so powerless when selling a house? Personally, it seems like Monopoly where I always ended up with the boot. The day I get the realtor's sports car is the day I'll be on a level playing field.

I only sold a house myself once, but I celebrate that marvellous experience, not expecting it to ever happen again.

The psychology of the family photograph

I wonder if anyone has done a thesis on the sociological or psychological implication of the family, school or community photograph. There are those perfectly poised and posed still where people are arranged according to height. Schools like that sort of thing, and some families appear to favour this style.

As for school photographs I don't remember any group photographs being taken at Avondale High where we were commonly referred to as Brown's Cows. Never was this more evident than when the Strathfield Sophisticates arrived on our patch for Sports Days, which were a complete nightmare for some, namely those who by reason of flexibility, height, athleticism or, in my case, total lack of motivation for the mad, sweaty rush and dash better demonstrated in gladiatorial Rome. Perhaps my personal aversion stemmed from the games of Brandy — an activity invented by the Marquis de Sade. One teacher was particularly enamoured of this frightful display of bullying in primary school. As we rushed from one end of the quadrangle to the other like wildebeests late for winter migration, Mr D would take aim, throw like Zeus, wounding and bruising herds of children as we fled and wept from the sting and wallop of the speeding tennis ball. While I lacked sportive assertion I possessed a high degree of outrage for this brutality. I may have been referred to on the odd occasion as incorrigible.

So pirouetted, ducked, weaved and leapt with nimble moves seen on no other occasion than when Mum had the suitcase strap and a head of steam. I hid behind the larger children, which was actually everyone else. I was often the last one left due to fierce determination to avoid sadism in all its painful forms. I would then inform Mr D that it was poor sportsmanship indeed to continue the debacle with only one child, not to mention that greater injustice of the teacher 'taking all the turns and never allowing students to 'brand' him.

So primary photos are rare. Other students might have them, but I have an assortment of childhood photos that defy description. In one, my mother had laid me as a babe on two mats, outdoors between two pot plants. In nearly all our infant photographs, my brother was crying. When questioned as an adult on the subject, he couldn't remember why.

What it Really Means to Be a Grownup

Making your own decisions means pleasing more people than ever before.

You actually receive MORE advice, not less, whether you asked for it or not.

You'd like to be mad at your parents for leaving you unprepared, but you remember them telling you every day that childhood was the best time of your life. Why you didn't realise THAT meant it was all downhill from there is down to you. Literally.

Paying the bills, cleaning up life's messes and doing your best doesn't come with brownie points, or even brownies.

The dentist doesn't give you balloons, just Sensodyne and dental floss. You visit doctors when you're not sick. Doctors don't give you lollypops, just bad news.

You realise that life often isn't about How You Play the Game. Life rewards the tossers, the racists and the warmongers. Those who build monuments to the great also build monuments to the stupid.

Being a grownup isn't what you thought it would be.

You realise that not fitting in means you're much better than you ever dreamed you could be.

Rundle Mall

The Adelaide chapters

Past the pale apricot stucco porticoed units with their square lawns and unpromising uniformity. Past the sprawl of schools, the diagonal stores with red-green awnings and hooded windows. Past the dust bowl kid's park with its faded grass. 'Do a U-turn - your destination is on the left,' google told me. But all I saw was a multi-storey carpark and the rear of what might be a magnificent building. The back façade was impressive. But there was no sign of coffee shops or restaurants. I didn't want to be late for Robyn, my new writing partner.

The sky above had that sun drenched haze that spoke of the beach, which was just over the low horizon of the paved esplanade. I drove into the lower level of the car park. 'Press the green button if you require parking' read the sign. Really! why the hell else would I venture in? This was all too complicated. I backed out, revving the engine and perhaps spinning a wheel or two. The solitary occupant of the paved esplanade, a caretaker with broom in hand and green slouch hat, saluted me with a grin. I returned the grin and gestured 'yes, I'm lost – what the heck'.

I parked near a line of neatly trimmed palms – not like the cocus crap, Syagrus romanzoffiana, I'd removed from my front yard. I asked a passerby for directions, and then a petite smiling assistant in a beautician's with glass-prism light and stunning product displays. She smiled warmly and pointed to a long line of storefronts just up the ramp. I started to walk briskly. Then, I looked up for the first time. And stopped. The ramp had risen over a marina.

The boats below, with their crisp, nautical tones of blue and dazzling white, gleamed with perfection. It was surreal to be above this azure vision, and yet so close. I stopped and breathed in the impossible beauty of it all. This new place. My place. And quite unexpectedly I caught a drift, a fragrant swell of possibility.

Maybe there is more to life than survival.

A very bad day

While I was walking down East Terrace in a ritzy suburb of Adelaide carrying two axes and kicking a box, I wondered who to blame for the shocking day I was having. George Pendlebury Smith aka GPS had been terribly imprecise with directions on the way to the real estate office to collect the huge pile of things the removalists had left behind. He'd told me to take the fourth exit at a T section that wasn't even a roundabout. Even though he never yelled (a character flaw I cannot tolerate in a man) I had moved from blaming myself for 'user error with technology' to being annoyed and experiencing a niggling doubt about his abilities.

I'd missed breakfast. I took the blame for that on the chin. When I put the last load of things into the car I noticed my legs were wobbling. Wobbling legs don't give one a lot of choice, they've gone from perfectly decent mobility units to total resistance in the blink of an eye. Even though driving doesn't require much of them, a red flag is raised to one inclined to over-utilise the accelerator. Logic kicked into my dehydrated little grey cells and diminished blood glucose levels screamed 'EAT! DRINK you moron!'

There was a café within walking distance – by now this meant a few short painful yards. The café was beautifully framed by shrubbery that was well under control. This fact alone informed that this was a suitable establishment. Everyone knows how I feel about vagrant hedges. This impression was further advanced when I saw the building. One entrance was marked MEMBERS ONLY. I stopped my imagination from running wild and decided NOT to ask what sort of club it was. I needed nourishment.

I entered. It looked more like a bar, but having good tolerance for embarrassment, I asked for a milkshake. (I'd seen it advertised on an ancient board near the bins outside). 'Don't get much call for that,' murmured the waiter. He offered a menu. I was overjoyed. Vittles as well, great! After the meal I informed him I needed The Ladies. It was that sort of establishment. No breezy 'Where's the loo, darl?' for this place. I was embarrassed to ask this. I can go days without needing The Ladies. Like a 'reverse camel'. I'm legendary for NOT getting up at night and NOT wandering shopping malls getting lost for days looking for bathroom facilities.

The Ladies was down a dark corridor. Into a dark hallway. Through a dark door that I found was actually a small foyer by feeling the walls. More wall exploration for the light switch. Through the next door. Repeat wall exploration. One loo. I vowed to be more sympathetic to my friends and relations when listening to their horrible experiences about public toilets.

On the drive home, fecking George Pendlebury Smith aka GPS instructed me to drive through an innocent looking Indian delicatessen and then expected me to drive on the railway tracks. A small car simply doesn't take on locomotives, even if it's red.

'Refugee' from NSW

It was embarrassing really. I've been in Adelaide for a year, and I hadn't been to Rundle Mall. I hadn't seen the famed golden orbs that can possibly be seen from outer space.

Having someone else drive me into the city took the worry out of getting lost in all the best suburbs with a diminished ability to enjoy their grandeur. But consumerism stilled hit me in the face as I headed down the mall. Does the human race really need this much 'stuff'? What does it all do? Is the majority of human endeavour now measured in making junk? And convincing us of our need for it?

I'd almost tired of the outing before it began. Then I heard the haunting lyric of a flute. It was narrating tales of long ago, of moss green valleys of peace, of water on smooth river stones, hinting at the timelessness of life. I followed the sound. A man sat, eyes closed in meditation. And played. Heedless of the coins thunking into the case in front of him. Lost in the magic with him, I looked at the people in the mall. There were no bustling anxious movements. Young people of many cultures leant on street stalls, waiting for the beneficence of French crepes, hot chocolate and other delights. Three wandering pigs were captured in bronze, amusing Japanese tourists who had headed for the LITTER bin and found instead a foraging bold swine with tilted ears.

Further, a young girl played a violin, elegant notes wove through the crowd with dextrous rapture. I heard the beat of drums and found it discordant to the setting. Until I saw that a young man had made plastic pipes into a source of music, and played the construct with a pair of thongs. The closer I came the more harmonious the rhythm seemed.

I found the golden orbs and turned to return down the mall. A boy with a guitar had replaced the violinist. And in the place of the flutist was a street performer, of the circus ilk. An energetic young Asian with bright eyes and the movements of a dancer. After each new trick he approached the audience and with extravagant emphasis sought their applause. They laughed and clapped their hands like awkward seals. An older man removed his hands from his pockets and joined the revelry.

I needed a rest in Myer. I slumped into a chair and watched. Sleek, exquisitely groomed women with sharp shiny stilettos glided the aisles of the cosmetics section. More stuff. A young man with eager smile and avant garde hair 'wishes to assist madam with foundation and powder choices'. Oh why not, okay. Madam agreed, allowing soft brushes and cool lotions to be applied in this season's new colours to texturise and moisturise. I am his blank canvas. He is pleased with his artistry. I glance at the mirror, madam is grateful, but madam is not a masterpiece. In fact, madam now seems as alive as the store dummies. But the skin tone coverage is even, so madam is grateful. After all, there's a price to pay for every seat in town.

Expiation

I looked forward to opening the yellow envelope. All my bills come by email now, so the angst of the letter box contents has faded. Seven letters fell out, all in a name I had the use of over two decades ago. Who could be that daft? They were official, with ornate government logos. They were also in another language – South Australian. As a (former) New South Welshman, this was confusing. 'Traffic', yes, understand that concept. But then 'expiation' – this was worrying. My last experience of that word had memories of overlong church sermons about sacrifice and temples. Expiation in those narratives meant you received something. I read a bit further and got goosebumps. I had speeding fines. In a former name. Which is why they weren't redirected with the rest of my mail but had done a circumnavigation of the country before arriving.

My first impulses included pushing the car off a cliff, burning it out in the bush or phoning the scrap metal guys. After all the fines were worth more than the car. I abandoned these ideas, not because they lacked merit, but because I'm one unlucky &^%$ and I'd end up hurting someone or causing an emergency event. And there was the VIN number. So I marshalled by high school debating skills and first convinced myself that their error should cancel out my transgression. Sadly this generous offer was not accepted by the 'Expiation Office'. In fact, its flawless delivery was met with silence then a jumble of words.

I phoned the RAA. Unlike the official channels Graeme was excited by my logic, and talked of affidavits and seeking the prosecution option. This was more like it. Courts offer a good day out. I got on so well with Graeme that I wouldn't have been surprised if he invited me around for tea to meet the family. 'Get photographic proof. They might have lost them, at the least it'll slow them down.' I liked his thinking.

Legal advice was the next obvious route. Community centres give it out free of charge. I sat opposite a sleek young thing and related my tale. She nodded and looked interested. 'So you see,' I said, 'I've been denied the opportunity to amend my behaviour because I didn't receive the first fine, because they put the wrong name on it. I mean if I'd received the first one I wouldn't have had the others...'

She burst out laughing. I was glad she hadn't been drinking her coffee at the time because I'd have worn it. 'That's beautiful,' she said, 'just beautiful. I love it. Unfortunately it won't fly anywhere.'

She suggested my Member of Parliament. I love going there too. Their secretaries are good value. I went to the wrong Member first, 'just go up *** Street and there's a big sign on the road outside,' said the assistant. I headed to the right Member. By now, half the State knew of my misfortune, or stupidity – depending on how you look at it. And the assistant had the appalling bad manners to grin at my tale of woe.

I arrived at the street. No sign. A woman was smoking outside in a covert 'I shouldn't be having a fag' kind of way and took pity on my obviously lost state. 'Up two flights and you can't miss it,' she said. I ran up two flights of stairs. I was at the Blood Bank. 'You're not bleeding me,' I thought and ran up two more flights of stairs. This assistant jumped on board, in spite of my criminal activities and offered to intervene. 'Don't write to them or contact them yourself,' she said, which didn't say much for my skills.

I phoned Graeme at the RAA again. We chatted like long lost relatives. His partner at the office, Tim, was a little less enthusiast. In fact he was downright reasonable. I'd received a flood of full colour portraits of the rear of my car, so I'd lost steam as well as my previous sense of entitlement. This could go very badly, and not for the Expiation Branch or my new friends at the RAA. 'So I should bend over and take it,' I said to Tim. 'Ah, well, yeah,' he said.

I relayed this to my son, affectionately known as The Manboy, when I visited. 'Geez, Mum you can't say that! That's terrible! You can't go around using that kind of language.' He wasn't the least bit interested in my explanation that our high school teacher, Mr Gilchrist had called the boys up to the front and whacked their rear ends with the blackboard ruler, causing a great deal of giggling that he was only too pleased to enjoy himself.

I'd been told I would have to go to Service SA. A daft name if ever I heard it – I mean the NAME tells you nothing, it could be a soup kitchen. There I would find out about demerit points, although I'd already googled *that* and cancelled my funeral fund, my Reader's Digest subscription and any pleasure I was planning for the rest of my life. Oh yes, and I'll be looking at pushbikes. Although I can see where that could lead!!!

I went to SA Service. Not a soup kitchen. In South Australia queues are a different animal. All the seating faces a large TV screen. Don't get excited, they flick ads for government departments.

The automated voice called out numbers. A blonde woman behind me swore. I laughed. She apologised.

'Oh please don't apologise,' I said, 'it's great to hear my native tongue in this foreign land.'

'Well they are fucking useless,' she said, 'I don't know why the place has *service* in the name.'

'I blame the internet,' said the Greek woman sitting next to me. 'That's the whole problem.'

'I'll kill the two of you,' said the blonde's husband.

'What? Both of us?' I asked.

'Oh sorry,' he said, 'I was talking to my dozey friends who don't know the difference between a debit and a credit VISA card.' 'This waiting business would drive you nuts.'

'Not as nuts as half a dozen speeding fines,' I said. He looked up and smiled sympathetically. 'They sent them in the wrong name.'

'Don't pay em,' he said.

'Throw them in the bin,' said the blonde.

'Well,' I said, 'they do have nice photographs of the rear of my car.'

'You're screwed then,' said the man.

'There's more cameras in this place than half Europe,' said the Greek woman.

Two or three people giggled. Another number was announced.

'So bloody slow,' said the blonde, clearly thinking of better places to be.

'They don't let you work for local government unless you can slow things down,' I said. Several more people giggled.

'I hate those cameras,' said the Greek woman, 'and the internet. Was alright before that.'

'I'd like to go and point the cameras towards the paddock. Let them take pictures of cows minding their own business,' I said. 'I can't wait to stop suddenly in front of a police car and when they hit me I'll tell them I was distracted by speed signs.'

The automated voice started calling numbers rapidly.

'They must have come back from lunch,' said the blonde. 'Wish I'd HAD some lunch.'

'A food truck would do well here,' I said.

My number came up. I handed in my rego plates and asked about my demerit points, or lack thereof. The service assistant frowned at the screen. 'You're not in the system.'

A stranger stranger

As I sat in my window seat on the plane I was too tired to feel apprehensive, too tired to introduce myself to the person next to me, so I closed my eyes.

I heard scratching and clicking and bumping. It sounded like the cat transfer I'd had to do the day before, but without the constant yowling. I opened one eye. The woman in the seat next to me was looking at herself in the mirror and clamping an eyelash curler on her lashes.

I was shocked. The plane hadn't even taken off. I could just see how badly that exercise could go if the plane jolted. The Band-Aid to fix *that* disaster hadn't been invented. I didn't want to look but I couldn't look away. I hoped the stewards knew what to do when someone's upper eyelashes had been yanked out by the roots. God only knows I wouldn't want the job.

The woman wriggled, preened then tapped the screen in front of her. I hadn't even noticed the screen. She was playing hangman, a little less dangerous than her former gymnastics with the eyelash curler. So I watched. Her movements were fast and furious, she was chewing gum as if there was a world shortage.

Then began the toilet visits. This was a difficult endeavour because the man in the aisle seat was snoozing and snoring, head lolling about. We'd only been in the air five minutes. I wish I could go to sleep like that. She woke him up, jostling and turning, apologising and fretting. By the time she came back he'd gone to sleep again. She shrivelled in embarrassment and tapped him lightly. He jumped. When she sat down she got the eyelash curler out again.

'Not feeling well?' I asked, hoping to take her mind off the dangerous sport of curling lashes.

'No, I have a stomach ache like you wouldn't believe. She squirmed and patted her stomach.

'Irritable bowel syndrome?' I asked.

'Yes, it's just horrible.'

'I know. It's awful.'

She was so relieved to find sympathy that she began to tell me about it. Thankfully not in great detail. She was much more interested in telling me that stress played a part and she'd had a godawful row with her husband/partner. He was in NSW at some conference or job, or perhaps both. She was flying up to surprise him.

My eyes widened. My tainted experience with partners of the husband variety told me that surprises were not always welcome.

Her stomach growled. 'I hate waking that poor Chinaman up,' she said, chewing her lip. She was going to be short one lip and a bunch of eyelashes if I didn't step in.

'I tell you what,' I said, with my registered nurse voice, 'the next time you go to the loo, I'll get the Chinese man to sit in my window seat so he won't be disturbed, we'll all shift up and you can have the aisle seat.'

She grabbed her stomach, it was clearly time for another visit. Snore, jerk, sorry, sorry. While she was gone, they were not short visits, I offered the man the window seat, he seemed grateful to be bossed around, even though he didn't seem to get the idea for a bit. He immediately slumped in the seat and leaned on the window. 'Do you want your pillow?' I asked quickly, wanting to catch him before he fell asleep at lightning speed again. 'Oh my thank you,' he said.

A stewardess came to investigate my shenanigans.

'She's not well,' I said gesturing in the direction of the toilet.

'Are you travelling together?' she asked politely.

'Oh no,' I said, 'I'm just organising her life.'

The eyelash curler came out several more times as she chewed tapped and fidgeted. I felt we were becoming best friends so I said, 'You're a bit hyperactive aren't you?' She didn't take offence at this, merely saying. 'God, yes! And I'm worse today – what with the fight with my partner and all'. Sometimes he was partner and other times husband. I thought it must be one heck of a row to fly across the country. In my experience men who'd just had rows or arguments were best left alone. It was my policy to not even follow an angry man into the next room, much less the next state or territory.

We were surprised to discover we'd be travelling on the same country train after the flight. Her stop was a few before mine on the long journey north from Sydney. I had to collect luggage at the carousel so she took off at speed. When I got on the northbound train there she was, sitting in the corner looking out the window like an anxious child. She turned and we laughed.

Over the journey her nervousness increased and the three other women in the carriage joined in, as women do. We heard about the husband, the row and the 'surprise' as she tried to read the names of the station. 'What sort of names are these? Ouuurimbaaah – is that aboriginal.'

I laughed, it was a relief for someone else to be the one mispronouncing towns. 'You're in NSW now,' I said, 'we don't pay undue attention to vowels – we grunt them out, it's pronounced 'arimba'.

The nervous routine continued, and the eyelash curler came out several times, astonishing the other occupants of the carriage.

'There are hundreds of stations, do we stop at all of them?' she asked.

'No, just a few.'

'What about Niagara, do we stop there?'

'It's Narara, and no,' said one of the woman with a grin, obviously a regular.

'The announcer voice thing is weak, I can't hear a thing. Mumble mumble, useless.'

'I'll tell you when to get off,' I said. 'Which station?'

'Tuggerah. Well, my husband said he'd meet me there, but knowing him...'

I exchanged a look with the woman opposite. Like me, she was a bit older, and the look in her eye said she'd had some experience with husbands, she was probably related to any number of people who had one.

She jumped up and headed for the door. 'Come and see me at the Warradale Hotel,' she said. 'We can catch up.'

'What's your name?' I yelled over the train noise.

'Susanne.'

'Bye,' I said. 'Good luck with...'

She was gone.

I saw a twinkle in the eye of the woman opposite. 'I wonder if he's there,' she said.

'I'll look,' I said, glad of chance to mind someone else's business.

I leaned towards the window, scanning the small station. I felt it only fair to give the others a running commentary. 'Nope, nope, can't see anyone like a husband, nope.' We flew past the station and I peered out the train window.

'Is he there? Is he there? Are there any likely looking men waiting?' asked the women.

'No, just one old geezer leaning on a walking frame.'

Second-hand, side-by-side refrigerator

Now she's yelling out of the front window, the old woman from the unit opposite who is seldom a reliable source of good humour.—'Get off the bloody grass! You idiot!' The man in the van has his windows up, to shut out the cold and rain—rain that's sheeting down with trenchant determination like an army on the march, oblivious. The driver is demonstrably oblivious, although he has the look of someone who may have practised the art of oblivion. His eyes are a little spacey, what can be seen of them through his dreadlocks, beneath the colourful beanie he wears like a Jamaican DJ.

The woman who arrived with him drags oily, thin hair behind her ears and tells me in a flat voice 'he's my partner. We're both on disability Ps.' I assume the P is pension - they only put 'DIS P' in the email. She informs me of this with an expectant air, as if this cruel act of life should reduce the already bartered-down price of the SIMPSON, 600L EXCELLENT CONDITION SIDE BY SIDE REFRIDGERATOR they've come to inspect. I ignore the hint - I'm not a fan of extended bartering and I don't really want to inform her that I'm also a DIS P. That might involve impairment comparison that could last until the Second Coming.

The old woman yells again. 'You bloody fool. You'll break the water pipes and we all know who'll have to pay up for that!' I cringe, feeling like a recalcitrant school kid. 'We all' don't actually know who'll have to pay, but I'm now guessing it's her, even though she's a tenant like the rest of us in the five unit complex. 'Senseless morons!' she adds, still in full voice.

The two DIS Ps eye the fridge as if it's Aladdin's cave, huge and abundant, but they shuffle and pretend indifference. They look it over. Van guy tosses his dreadlocks and clears his throat, talks about needing 'that kinda space, but...' They want to barter but lack the assertion. The woman points at a tiny mark that could be an eyelash. I shrug. 'We need a new fridge because my other partner sold the house.' I have no inkling or desire to follow the destination offered by this statement. They stare for so long I wonder if they want me to offer to let them have a little time alone with the fridge, to bond with it, check it out, see if it's compatible.

Dreadlocks hands me the money, brings the trolley, and they both muscle the huge thing out of the kitchen, across the carpeted lounge room, out the front door down the step, up the path, across the grass, up the ramp, onto the trailer.

Vigilante Tenant Wreaks Havoc

"The body corporate for a block of flats in Adelaide is in hot water today because of the action of a 61 year old woman at the end of her patience. Armed with pruning shears and a hand-held tree saw, the woman trimmed the overgrown hedge that, due to its length and weight, had grown, then fallen across the tenant pathway. Several weeks after the branches collapsed, in spite of the attendance of a yard maintenance guy, the overhanging branches had not been pruned. The body corporate mandate is to only attend hedge reduction twice a year.

"However the hedge hasn't been pruned for 18 months. The overhang of the hedge onto the path is six feet from the fenceline and has normal traffic of up to 20 persons per day. The hedge protrudes so far across the walkway that only several inches of the path is usable.

"The roots from the hedge have long been a source of contention and worry for tenants. They have caused cracks and raising of the cement path, creating a significant safety hazard—making an accident a matter of when not if. Equally worrying is the fact that the hedge is an entire ecology system. However, it's hard to imagine a world where huge rats are an endangered species or a necessary part of the environment. I could be wrong. I was back in 1984. Twice.

"This situation raises some interesting questions. What are the ramifications for a tenant who takes matters into their own hands? Can this type of vigilante action be tolerated in today's society?

"The woman remains unrepentant and merely states that she is pursuing avenues for lawsuits for rashes, grazes and injury to her person because of the inability of a governing body to exercise due diligence. Will further injury occur? Will there be a class action? Will the rat population decrease? And, God forbid, will the civic minded woman be reprimanded or penalised for her actions? She is currently accessing data on visiting regulations for the local penitentiary."

Vigilante Tenant – Part II

The yard maintenance guy came. He stood perplexed at the huge pile of branch debris. It was an organised pile so there hadn't been a storm. He looked at his trailer and assessed it as inadequate for the task. I pitied him. So I confessed. I mean if it's good enough for George Washington... Yes, I cut the hedge. In my defence, it was already more than half 'down'. At this stage I'd only given it a light trim. However I'd underestimated the hedge. Merely removing the leafy foliage had left what looked like a wall of spikes worthy of a Monty Python episode. This was a hedge that did now go lightly into that dark night.

After a nice chat with Zeke the yard guy, I decided to confess to Rob, the CEO of the Strata Title Company. I'd already met him and had a wonderful yakathon. Rob was so impressed with my concerns that he told me to hand the phone to Zeke and said, 'Do whatever Linda says and send us the invoice'. Well, poor Zeke. Imagine. After a stunned silence Zeke spoke. The job was too big for him. The overgrowth required more than his usual hedge trimming equipment.

Naturally that required the services of an arborist with at least two quotes. And quite naturally, that was my responsibility. So I phoned two certified companies. The quotes were hideous. The receptionist at the Body Corporate had a fit. No permission for rectifying the problem was forthcoming. So I cut more growth back.

I was beginning to harbour strong feelings of hostility for the hedge. I was fair sick of walking past it and seeing a rat or three tripping gaily through the branches at eye level, while his friends and relations scurried in the leaf litter at the bottom that smelt like a rat sewer. Which it was. I named it 'Deadly Boa Constricticis Enormi' then googled it. It was a *Ficus pumila*, commonly known as Creeping Fig. It can grow on cement, glass, and Balinese temples with ease, often destroying the building as it grows. This hedge had wound through the cement work of the fence and cracked whole section of the fence, something that couldn't be seen before I trimmed back the excess. The vine has purple pear-shaped fruit, which is described as *'not high on the edibility list and barely squeaks in'*

After one of my friends with severe arthritis tripped on the cracked path, I decided to go all out and trim it precisely to the fenceline. Sadly this meant that the weight of the vine on the other side of the fence capitulated to gravity. The back yard of the neighbour was covered in ficus pimula debris. The neighbour who held loud outdoor parties on weekends that started at 2pm in the afternoon and ended at 3am. The pleasure derived from the party goers, apart from copious imbibing of alcohol, seemed to be singing along loudly to football songs.

The woman in the unit opposite, who'd been lamenting the state of the hedge one week prior cornered me in the yard to yell at me. This is a much-enjoyed pastime of hers, and she targets primarily those who drive on the lawn, or put things on the lawn. Well, do anything at all to the lawn really. She said she was going to deal with this and phone Rob.

'Of you go then,' I said, which must have been a less than satisfactory response because her daughter knocked on my door the next day and gave me another style of loud advice that began with, 'what the hell were you thinking? You've ruined the fence and devalued all our properties. Besides that hedge is the natural habitat for the Native Fruit Rat'. 'I think you'll find it's closer to the Rat that Caused the Black Plague in the Dark Ages,' I said.

'I *liked* you, Linda,' she said, hands firmly on hips, squarely putting any friendly sentiment towards me in the past tense.

To this day the word 'rat' cannot be uttered around either of my sons without sparking great hilarity and entertainment. As the eldest said, 'there's no such thing as a native fruit rat'.

The day after that the neighbour from Party Central knocked on my door.

'Do you know why I'm here?' he said.

'You've come to yell at me. You're the next in the queue, I'm guessing.'

He gave a wry, deflated smile. He lamented his exposed backyard and said, 'we're very private people, Linda.'

'Could've fooled me, Mark,' I said. 'I wouldn't have thought that people who value privacy would sing drunk karaoke all night long outside for the world to hear.' I paused. 'Shattering the privacy and peace of every neighbour for at least two blocks.'

He looked sheepish. 'Yeah. Righto. I've had anonymous notes in my letterbox.'

'Hmm,' I said pointedly.

There were no more loud parties for the rest of my tenancy. And when I saw Mark crouched under a small umbrella in his small yard with stacked party chairs, and a deconstructed party gazebo, smoking a cigarette and reading the newspaper, I didn't care one bit. So I wrote a poem...

'Twas the night before Christmas, when all thro' the house
not a creature was stirring, not even a mouse.
And rattus rattus, that's common Black Rat to you
has fled the scene with friends one thousand and two.
With nary a one to put its twitching nose near a trap.

Nonetheless, all the neighbours remain in a flap.
While they have conceded, with reluctant pity
that 'native fruit rats' have not graced this fair city
for a century or more, preferring rural locale—
and at the sight of fruit they turn rather pale.

The children were nestled all snug in their beds,
While visions of sugar plums danc'd in their heads.
And still, in spite of Christmas, good cheer, and Saint Nick
there's plenty of time for the throwing of bricks
into red bins or green, whatever is near.

'The Council won't mind, be assured, never fear,'
says he who is scarcely familiar with rules,
who sneaks in the night with dubious tools.
Then sends a text message to those near and far,
'Blame Linda, here's her details, there's no bar
to phoning or knocking 'ere you please—or just call
to ask why the dickens she caused the hedge to fall.'

When out on the lawn there arose such a clatter,
I sprang from the bed to see what was the matter.
Along with the demolition of mortar and fence
a lone Skip Bin arrived, it was truly immense.
In this season of rejoicing the lament rose even higher.

The Sacred Lawn God has again been defiled.
The bin's ugly blue presence caused quite a stir;
feathers flew, and, well, even some fur.
The queue grew ever longer to my front door
not Good Tidings of Joy, of that I am sure.

Away to the window I flew like a flash,
Tore open the shutters, and threw up the sash.

There on my doorstep appeared a fairly decent fellow
who, unlike the others, was seasonably mellow.
He wanted to yell, but offered restraint.
I looked in my dotage, perhaps I might faint.
He pointed slowly in mute frustration
at the debris of sticks, the hedge devastation.

As dry leaves before the wild hurricane fly,
When they meet with an obstacle, mount to the sky.
Why, or why, did I undertake such an infraction?
Whatever possessed me to take such action?

With amused patience I quoted the law
I'd gained permission long before
The Govt Health site was enlightening, I said
Wherever more than a few rats lay their heads
it's called 'squalid and substandard living conditions'
'Thanks goodness,' I said, 'the law makes provision.'

And while others might be fond of the rustle of leaves
as rats pass by, dining alfresco as they please,
returning at night to a warm bed of excrement
Had he not smelt the acrid aroma that meant?

The moon on the breast of the new fallen snow,
gave the lustre of mid-day to objects below.
'But Linda, we value our privacy, and now we have none
Do you see, do you know, what you have done?'

'I do mate, truly I do, but can you please explain
how your all night loud parties with boozy refrain
align with the concept of privacy. Mate, I'm confused!'
He flushed, stood quietly, a little bemused–
'But Linda, but Linda, that's not a light trim!'

He looked so crestfallen I took pity on him,
'It's more a Brazilian, I do understand, mate.
I can see the aesthetic isn't that great.'

A wink of his eye and a twist of his head
Soon gave me to know I had nothing to dread.

He arrived the next day, the Skip Bin his hire.
He was targeted then, and faced the dread ire
of owners and managers, relative and friend.
He sighed and placated, would there be no end?

He faced the distress of all till he was worn
Answering those weeping for the death of the lawn.

With placating tones – he said, 'Don't think twice
I sincerely promise it'll be gone in a trice
I had no choice but to put the Skip there
but, the lawn won't die, I'm taking great care.'

More rapid than eagles his helpers, they came,
And he whistled, and shouted, and call'd them by name.

Soon his heaving, dismantling and toil was done
the Skip Bin disappeared, evening had come.
But there, in dawn's pale light, like blow to the head
a rectangle of brown – the lawn is dead.

So this Yuletide Eve I'll stay out of sight
Happy Christmas to all, and to all a good night.

I am tenant no more. Vigilante no longer. Have I put my pruning shears down? Not exactly. Having bought my own home in the Barossa I have sent trailer loads of pruning debris to the tip. Happily, without murmur or complaint from a single living soul. My two sons, now accustomed to my Do or Die gardening style have merely shaken their heads, grinned and shared stories of What Mad Thing Mum Did This Week. However, whenever I make the 70km journey and pass my former abode, they've told me I could at least have a quick LookSee at the hedge, and give them an update. But, I didn't want to face my former neighbour, the woman who yells at anyone who venturing onto the lawn. She is always watching. She has a wide window overlooking the yard and carpark that her family calls her "television", so keen is she to monitor comings and goings. I was reluctant. So I didn't.

Until I had a quick trip down to Marion. The words of my youngest son tickling my brain—"if you had enough guts to take down a whole hedge, upset homeowners and strata bodies, then what's the big deal about taking a look. I want photos." His traitorous brother concurred with a wicked grin. So I did.

The once unmanaged hedge is now trimmed meticulously. While the stain from rat excrement can still be seen, it's obvious the body corporate intents that hedge won't go wild again. Not on the unit complex side anyway. It is mere millimetres from the cement fence. No room at all for fat grey rats to nod polite acquaintance to you as they scamper at eye level when you pass by.

India? How long?

At the Post Office an Indian woman was seeking to send a parcel to India and having difficulty with the genial Postmaster.

'But India,' she said, 'how long?' Her smooth brown arms gave urgent emphasis as they made circles in the air.

'India, I can't say. There are no guarantees for India.' The calm attendant shrugged his shoulders and smiled.

'Surely, but India—how long?

'I can't tell you India. Every other country I can say. But India, I can't say.'

'But surely. If I post today, how long?' Her petite body leaned over the post office counter.

He sighed, his eyes quickly assessed the long queue of customers yet to be served.

They both looked of Indian descent. Maybe they spoke the same language. I wondered if that would assist the woman's understanding. It didn't.

I left my position as third in the queue. After all, this nonsense had been going on for ages, showing no sign of resolution. I decided to address the postbag, write the note and then pay. I was getting annoyed anyway.

A man had jumped the queue, slanting himself behind a woman of generous proportions. The tilt of his head and the squaring of his shoulders told me he meant to stay put. It's the city. Queue-jumping is an expected assertion, unlike small country towns where it's in everyone's best interests to get along.

'But if I post to India, post today, surely you must know when ... maybe ten days?'

'Reeeally, I don't have a clue, really.' He sighed, his patience untrammelled. 'If I fly to India to deliver the parcel, then ten days I guarantee. Postage—I can't say.'

Lily pilly

Avant

I remember sitting on the rim of the universe, dangling my legs. Waiting. For that gentle angel-shove off the bench at the door to heaven.

The boy sitting beside me looks a little worried. 'Do you think we'll be angels or devils on earth?'

'Oh!' I say. (it's a question I hadn't considered).

'Both, I guess,' I say, shrugging.

'Will there be Maths I wonder,' he muses.

I shudder.

The others on the bench are squirming now. Their minds are winding back, ticking like miniature metronomes, back to the almost-zero state of mind necessary to be born on earth.

'Stop shoving,' one says.

I exchange a look with the boy. He shakes his head. 'That doesn't bode well,' he says.

The angel comes; the one that pushes us off into the cosmos.

'Why do we have to be pushed?' asks the boy.

'It prepares you for life on earth,' says the angel, standing in front to deliver a last few words to each of us.

'Linda.' The angel uses my earth name, as her wings flutter to her sides, and remain still as midnight.

'Yes. Do I get some other names?'

'You ask too many questions,' says the boy.

I give him the 'who's being a hypocrite look now' look.

'You might,' says the angel, 'it's up to the parents you're born to.'

'They seem nice,' I say, peering down. 'Are they?'

The angel stretches out a wing so I can't see. That doesn't perturb me. 'They've never given up on each other, they're not the type to give up on a kid ... child,' I say, pushing my luck. We're not supposed to ask for reassurances. It's a trust thing.

The angel sighs. 'They'll probably give you a name of someone who's really special to them.'

'So Pocohontas is out then.' I mutter, wondering why no one else is asking questions.

'They'll like me,' I say, to no one in particular. 'They've waited ages for a girl. Especially the mother person.'

'You won't be exactly what she expects.' The angel's wings begin a fluttering tremor. When she speaks again, I struggle to keep my alert mind, not the baby one that's taking over. 'Is anyone up for...?' she asks.

Then I, in my ignorant bliss, say, 'Sure, I will!'

The next thing I know, we're falling, although it's more like a drift. I turn to the boy, 'Did she ask if anyone was up for three lifetimes in one?' I ask.

But the boy is sucking his thumb, his mind has slipped to where it should be.

'Bother,' I say, wondering why it's taking so long for my baby brain to kick in.

Home

Max, my father, had been an engineer. A handsome man, tall and spare of frame with twinkling eyes that set off his gentle face. His jet black hair had receded early lending him a professorial air. With a serious nature he was deeply committed to his spiritual convictions. He was thorough and patient, cautious and cool-tempered. He had indulged in his share of mischief as a child but had matured into a quiet and thoughtful adult. His humour was dry and ironic and bordered on sarcasm. Dad was a technical genius and designed machinery that was flawless in detail, often repairing things for other people for very little extra cash. One day he smilingly brought home a pumpkin that had been given as pay for his extensive work, donated by the richest man in town. When his pet rabbit died I found him crying alone and disconsolate behind the outside dunny.

Elsie, my mother, was a 'stenographer'. She had gorgeous hair and great legs. Woefully short sighted, she wore heavy dark-framed glasses. She was in her own eyes, a plain Jane. She summed herself up by saying, 'You can't make a silk purse out of a sow's ear'.

I was born late according to the apparently infallible due date that the doctor had deemed would be my time of arrival. This was a practice that I continued for most of my life and was oft commented on by my mother who was prone to say about this habit, 'Linda would be late for her own funeral.'

Although a little bleary because of a generous application of 'the mask' she heard the Doctor say, 'It's a girl and she is perfect'. This particular fact my mother would dispute for the rest of her life. The Doctor applied a swift slap to my bum as was the custom of the day in order to make me breathe. My mother continued this practice enthusiastically for the first 12 years of my life in order to stop me from breathing so that she would not have to listen to the constant torrent of words that came from my unruly mouth.

'That girl has been infected with a gramophone needle', she would often say referring to the technical apparatus of the day that supplied you with noise all day long. Of course the gramophone supplied music and I fell quite short of any musical talent but this was deemed by her to be a fitting description of my garrulous nature. I was joyful and spontaneous because the world I had arrived in made complete sense to me and I was filled with both fascination and enchantment with each new adventure and each new person who entered my world. This was not so for my mother. The world did not make sense for her because she lived on an alien planet. Planet Autism.

My mother was 36 and her short wavy brown hair had not a whisper of grey. At my birth she had produced a pigeon pair, which meant one of each sex. She was elated at her success in this regard and was even more proud that she had first produced a son and then a daughter. So, in the true English style that she upheld she had produced an heir and then a girl. This achievement gave her no end of pride and no-one could ever convince her that this arrangement had nothing to do with her but was controlled by nature.

My mother was a social climber without a ladder. The fact that my parents were actually quite poor and didn't even own a car which effectively meant there was no dynasty for the heir did not detract from my mother's pride in the marvellous order of the arrival of her children. Perhaps she thought the dynasty would arrive one day. Or perhaps having been raised with the severe and relentless work ethic of the country folk of the 1930's she believed that good hard work would supply her with the eventual justified reward of prosperity.

Even though reality did not supply her very much in the way of material goods she managed to pretend that the abundant life was just around the corner. So her life was a constant struggle to inch her way up the social ladder. This firm belief in imminent prosperity caused her to overdo everything. If she did not achieve prosperity it would not be because she did not deserve it, and to deserve it she must apply every thought and muscle to physical work of some kind. It was an obsession.

Our home reflected this in every 'nook and cranny'. The copious gardens that edged every side of the house were designed to require the kind of attention that could have only been supplied by several gardeners but my mother was up to the challenge. She applied the kind of drive and physical effort that made the TV gardening program Backyard Blitz look like kindergarten. She was an unstoppable force of nature. A one woman army. The basic premise seemed to be the harder you made your life the more deserving you must be. Every inch of the garden was crammed with some kind of plant life creating a cacophony of smells rather than a fragrant ambience. In tune with her workaholic ethic she planted annuals as well as perennials and chose the most difficult plants to grow. I'm sure she made determined efforts to obtain plants that were not suited to the climate or conditions of our area and believed that they would prosper by the sheer force of her considerable will. They didn't. Even though she placed plastic bags nightly over the tropical plants all through winter to protect them from the killing frosts they never flowered although they survived, stunted and mute. She especially loved frangipanis and even though she was singularly unsuccessful with them she never allowed herself to give up on them. She would prevail.

My parents were quite fond of leisurely drives around the lake and surrounding neighbourhood and I don't ever remember a time when we went on a drive that she didn't compare the size of all the frangipani trees she saw and whether they were laden with blossoms. She deeply resented those gardeners who had been more successful in the matter of frangipanis than she had. It was a trial to her but also a scourging goad to make her try even harder and invest in whatever new fertilizer would promise gardening success. It never seemed to occur to her that the frangipanis that did flourish grew near the gentler climate of the lake thus escaping the deadly frost.

We lived in a house that was typical of the houses of our neighbours. Unlike the current trend in the area where old weatherboard houses with disreputable exteriors sit side by side with brick and tile double storey masterpieces. Our house was a big square white weatherboard. It was not permitted to fade like those of our neighbours. It wouldn't have dared. However all of her days in this house my mother was offended by weatherboard. She belonged in brick and tile and life had cruelly not only dished up weatherboard but the rear of the house was fibro and this further increased her resentment towards the house. Unable to move up in the world and to another area of town she put her considerable energy into pressuring my father to 'do the house up'. No amount of doing up ever took it as far up as she wished it to go.

I found this process very confusing as a child because it didn't appear to me to be a case of actually improving anything but merely rearranging. And this was the time of my mother's burgeoning love affair with anything garishly orange or lurid lime green. The master bedroom became the kitchen and with the extraordinary logic known only to my mother this was achieved by actually using the same kitchen cupboards and appliances. My opinion on this matter was given and it was swiftly enforced on me that my opinion had not been sought and was indeed not required. I was a child. What would I know of the world of 'grown ups'? If the twinkle in my father's eye betrayed his consensus with me it was not spoken out loud. For he quite justly feared that he would receive precisely the same advice that I had been given. Apparently we were both children. He was just a more useful and pliable child than I was. So the laundry with the copper became the bathroom and then with the arrival of the new Westinghouse automatic washing machine it became the laundry again. It still contained all the bathroom essentials so I was quite at a loss to know what to call it as we already had another bathroom that had once been a large broom closet.

Our house was also similar to many others of the time in that rooms had been added in a completely random fashion and had often originally been constructed without any council approval. So inch by inch the law was flouted in our neighbourhood. Some houses had so many rooms tacked on that the original house was completely swallowed up. The usual practice was to add a verandah, then put a roof over it and then wall it in. The same was done to carports. As there was a university nearby and a large factory the purpose for these enlargements was quite often for the purpose of renting out a portion of the house to supplement the family income. It was before the time when rooms were added for parents' retreats, play rooms, teenage retreats and ensuites. If you needed the loo while someone else was there you were simply told to cross your legs, shut up and buzz off.

We had an outside dunny like most others and were disturbed weekly by the night cart rattling down the street and the 'dunny man' stomping through yards in the wee hours of the night disturbing the well earned rest of working men and dogs alike. Our first toilet paper consisted of newspaper torn into sheets and shoved on a three inch nail. I was about twelve when we became the proud owners of the inside toilet. After that time my mother resolutely refused to believe or admit that we had ever possessed a dunny. Whole family gatherings could become quite tense affairs if one of our unsuspecting cousins happened to remark casually that 'no matter how poor they were as children they were at least spared the indignity of the outside dunny'. My brother and I learned to leave that subject well and truly alone in public though we had many a chuckle on the side.

The outside dunny prepared you for life in ways that an inside toilet could never achieve. The mere act of venturing outside in the middle of the black night was enough to give courage to the faintest heart. Or added fear to the already terrified soul that deemed a chamber pot under the bed a necessity. There was never a 'pot' in our house as my mother said she would rather 'crawl through hell on her hands and knees than own one of those things'. I was quite pleased with this decision on her part due to my propensity to 'put my foot in it' in so many other areas of life. And not even my mother wanted to clean 'one of those'. So we took the path of fear. The added danger of the possibility of meeting a snake or a redbacked spider or tripping over something and landing headlong in the dunny hole filled me with utter dread. Of course you tried to carry a torch but while you were ensconced on the seat, which often moved and pinched your bum, it was very difficult and ineffective to control the beam of light. At night my terror usually had me squatting near the back door in the light from the kitchen window to pee on the grass. This proved quite satisfactory until one night my brother's dog Snoopy arrived quietly and showed his pleasure at finding me by licking my bum. This event scarred me for life and my deep humiliation was only dissipated by the fact that for once in my inelegant and curious childhood I did not have an audience or punishment. So I went back to the dunny, the torch and my fears of the local wildlife.

With her obsession for order my mother was always 'requesting' that my father put in cupboards. So every room contained at least one large cupboard. And in preparation or perhaps the pretence of the abundant life every cupboard was chock full of stuff. I don't know why we ever had a garbage bin because my mother never threw anything out. Wrapping paper was prepared for reuse and then never used. Having been a secretary before her job as a shop assistant at the local corner food store my mother had a love of paper and writing equipment. In light of this fetish one whole side of the spare room cupboard was set aside for this purpose, writing pads of every size and description, lined and blank, carbon papers, pens, inks etc, even though I never knew my mother to actually correspond with anyone except for those who had raised her ire and goaded her to reprove them or argue about a bill or fee for services.

My mother's compulsion for cleaning everything within an inch of its life also included the cupboards. My assistance was required. 'Linda, take everything out and clean and dust the shelves'. I was both appalled and overwhelmed. I could not conceive of how any dirt or even a speck of dust could fit in along with the other contents, especially under them. And I never understood why dusting was required prior to cleaning. So I usually banged around hoping to achieve 'efficient' noises and made things look a little different, waited a reasonable interval and then proudly called out for her to come and inspect my 'handiwork'. She always had to inspect things thoroughly. I would hold my breath, cross my fingers and toes and live in fear until I got the grunt of approval or the swat of the back of her hand and the inevitable, 'Hopeless, do it again!'

The linen cupboard was the biggest challenge. I think my mother had bought precisely the same number of towels that her mother had for eight children and two adults in the home of her childhood. We had at least sixty for the four of us. When I was told to take these out and dust and clean my fear went up several notches. This malarkey always turned out the same. She would always plunge her hand into the back and emerge with dust on it so no amount of pretending would get me out of this one with my usual antics of not actually cleaning. When the three piles of towels were in the cupboard they were each a foot tall, squashed neatly taking up the whole height and breadth of the cupboard. However when you took them out each pile had swollen to two and a half feet tall and each pile had grown a couple of inches wider. This phenomenon confused the hell out of me.

The cleaning and dusting were achieved relatively easily. But the real struggle began when it was time to return the now larger piles of towels to the cupboard. I could never do it. I squashed and pummelled and puffed and panted but nothing on earth would make those bloody towels fit back in the way my mother had arranged them. Any one who has ever put towels away knows that the best way to do it is usually one at a time. This did not work with my mother's system. I always had about two towels left over out of each pile that would not go in the cupboard. Making matters worse was the fact that the piles now had a decidedly squashed appearance and didn't even fit neatly sideways much less contain the original number. I usually gave up early on this endeavour as the punishment for this disaster was usually only verbal as it gave my mother a much enjoyed opportunity to show her superiority in all things domestic in a dramatic fashion. She would arrive on the signal of my much rehearsed pathetic bleating and with great flourish show me just how it was done. With none of the panting and exhaustion that accompanied my efforts her strong square hands would compress the towels into the designated place with a satisfied humph.

I used to like to think that the towels had just cowered in defeat and given up like I had done. The pleasure my mother received from showing me this wonderful skill was enhanced by my humble and grovelling praise, also much rehearsed. So this was one of the few occasions where there was no swat or emphatic declaration of my hopelessness in all things domestic along with her sincere wish that I never married and tormented some poor husband and children of my own.

Of course I could *never* repeat her skill with the towels, even after many demonstrations and I often considered throwing a few towels in the bin or donating them to the local charity on the sly. But the anxiety that this thought triggered reminded me of the time that I had tried to dispose of some of the less than appetising salad ingredients from my dinner plate. I had worn an apron to the table and on several occasions put finely chopped lettuce, beetroot and the even more finely grated carrot into my apron pocket. I was desperate as I seemed to be able to able to chew this stuff for hours but was strangely incapable of swallowing it. My sincere and tearful protestations explaining this difficulty gained me no sympathy only a single pithy 'nonsense' from my mother. So on the pretence of the visit to the dunny I would deposit the discarded vegetable slush into the garden. This was an extremely successful venture until I forgot the outside visit and garden depositing and the apron ended up in the wash. I think it was the bloody beetroot stain through the clothes in the washing machine that sealed my doom.

I was not a success at deception but this did not mean I didn't give it my best shot. We children had been told quite forcefully never to swing on the clothesline but in the days when there were no parks with slippery dips or spinning contraptions the clothesline was as close at it came to the ultimate temptation on a slow listless sunny day. One day the boy across the road and I were tempted beyond our meagre self control and convinced ourselves that no one would ever know, after all not *every* dire threat of impending doom from parents came true. We succumbed and had about the most fun I have ever had in the few squealing hours of bliss that the clothesline spinning afforded us. We eventually tired of this sport and our energy spent we sat on the back steps satisfied and content. Our bliss continued until we gazed at the instrument of our enjoyment and to our shock and dismay, while two of the arms of the clothesline were still true and straight the other two were bent earthwards in a curved and hideous fashion. Oh dear, we were for it now! Our bums tingled in anticipation of the warming they would receive when the parents came home to certain discovery of our vandalism. There was no way we were going to be able to cover this disaster up. After lengthy deliberations and various pathetic attempts to push the arms back up John conveniently realised that my mother would be home soon and made a hasty escape to his place as he feared my mother more than his own. But there would be punishment for us both, he would suffer at his house and I at mine. I was silently wishing that we had chosen his parents clothesline as she was not nearly as fierce with the bum whacking as my mother but more expressive with the words, most of which were prefaced with 'you bloody kids again'. We actually found her ire hilarious and would listen outside the window to her 'ear-bashing' of her current victim. She had six children so her patience must have been severely tested daily. Her emotional venting was only matched by her large hearted attitude to us all so we forgave all insults hurled our way.

The tortuous cleaning processes at our house also involved the windows. Well really they actually featured the windows as these were most readily seen by all. Her usual method of masochism prevailed and she insisted on venetian blinds, sheer drapes and then heavy drapes and these were all religiously positioned at precise times of the day and night. Early morning meant the opening of the blinds and pulling back of the heavy curtains. I never minded this at all as it was a ritual that gave her pleasure and more importantly never involved my participation. The cleaning of the whole lot was another matter entirely. The venetians had to be removed by the tallest and most technical child, that being my father. Then they were hung from the clothes line where it was my job to 'scrub every inch of them'. To add to my torment Ford's dog, Snoopy the bum licker of my previous dunny adventures was left tied to the clothesline to further add nuisance to the task. The cleaning of the venetian blinds was high adventure for Snoopy but caused great wrath and resentment in me. No matter how I protested about his presence, Snoopy was allowed to be wherever Ford wanted him.

My mother's death wish for my pets didn't apparently include Ford's dog. I guess being the heir had advantages. Snoopy was Ford's 16th birthday present. He was reputed to be a cross between a dachshund and an Alsatian. Many theories on his conception were put forward and raucously chuckled over by Ford and his friends but not in front of my mother for fear of the tongue lashing for having a 'filthy mouth'. In the genetic struggle for Snoopy's appearance it seemed the dachshund had won out as Snoopy had short legs and long ears that trailed the ground and a furious pointy little tail. The Alsatian evidence was there however as he was huge, he looked for all the world like a dachshund on steroids. Snoopy, like most dogs had a great and lifelong love of any kind of dirt. He was even the muddy red-brown of East Australian soil.

Against all logic my mother actually appeared to have a certain fondness for Snoopy as he was allowed inside on occasion where he nervously and energetically skidded, scraped long doggy toenails and slipped sideways on the floors and knocked over my mother's indoor pot plants. This did not cause the same fury that was aroused upon the arrival of my cat draped lovingly over my arm when I tried the same trick. Snoopy was funny. Even when he ripped the edges of her best sheets he was hilarious. Any mention on my part of the unfairness of this earned me the expostulated remark that 'my cats piddled'. It just wasn't worth reminding her that Snoopy had occasionally left a well placed turd on her preciously shiny pristine floors.

The processes of cleaning involved more chemicals than were ever used in any factory or hospital. Our weekly shopping venture contained as many cleaning products as it did items of food. Every different surface required a specialised product. And they were usually in the form of aerosols. One for polishing timber, sparkling glass, mirror finish for metal, Ajax for tiles, Exit Mould for the shower and on the list went. Unable to believe anything that was said face to face from another human being my mother embraced every cleaning advertisement ever made. We never knew whether the house would smell of pine, lavender, sandalwood or citrus. She was invincible to the effects of these chemicals and never wore gloves and scoffed at me when I showed her reddened hands and protested that I would cough my lungs up if I had to be shut in the shower with the Exit Mould one more time. I managed to avoid poisoning myself with the fumes by another route that involved deception as I would enthusiastically scrub the walls with the kitchen scourer and just before she arrived to inspect the shower I would spray a well-placed squirt of Exit Mould right where her nose would enter the shower. I should feel regret for my deceitful antics but I still have my sense of smell and taste so that has taken the edge off any regret or twinge of conscience I might otherwise have suffered.

She however did pay this price later but as usual the rest of us paid a greater price. She lost her sense of smell and taste. So then the overly bland food of before became excessively salted and her love of all things sweet went through the roof. We teased her that she would add sugar to water. But the worst of our suffering was that her use of perfumes, sprays and chemicals was increased so she could attempt to smell them. Whenever I saw her I was blasted back towards the front door by whatever new perfume she was wearing. I asked her politely what the perfume is called.

'Mum,' said my oldest son, 'it isn't perfume it's called fumes and it is **Channel** No 5'.

A hungry childhood

My tripping, stumbling journey through childhood was a quest, not just for answers but for acceptance and the kind of love that didn't change when you messed up. As a child I had an empty space, a hungry childhood. A place that had been created by the constrictions and harshness of a mother confined in a narrow, rule-bound world. She knew no other way, no other love. Sometimes when I watched her relentless activity I saw a glimpse of her own white-knuckled fear, as she dealt with her anxieties and emotions. I later learned that she had suffered crippling Post Natal Depression after the birth of my brother and was terrified of parenthood.

No-one has come from a vacuum. We make much of inheriting the colour of our eyes, our physical form and our talents, but we don't want to talk about our gifted emotional landscape, even though it is as much a part of who we are as our skin colour or temperament. Why if we were raised speaking Spanish then it would be perfectly natural to respond every time we hear someone speak Spanish. It would resonate deep within and we would be drawn instinctively to someone who spoke our mother tongue.

We wonder why we are drawn to people or situations later in life when it is really quite simple. We have heard a timeless lyric that is buried deep in our psyche. We may not know why, but we respond unerringly like a compass to magnetic north. We sense home. It may not be wise or beneficial but it makes perfect sense to seek the familiar.

Confusion was the Houston, from which I was launched. It was the story that built my realities and created my fantasies. It was not only confusion but also fear. Fear because I didn't understand, fear because I couldn't ask questions and the pervading fear of getting it all wrong.

Physical punishment was frequent and unpredictable, often sudden and brutal. I was never sure why as I didn't know what I had done to deserve such brutality. I never showed anger, lied to them, came home late or missed my homework. The only things I understood was that I disordered her world, was forgetful and couldn't do my chores as well as she did them. I failed her impossible standards. There weren't any calls from school about my behaviour. If I had problems with other children or school, it was very rare for me to share those difficulties as I feared further punishment.

'If we got into trouble at school, when we arrived home Mum gave us double what we had at school,' Mum would often say. Discretion seemed the better part of valour.

Before Mum started full time work, when I was a preschooler and Peter had started school, she would be 'at the end of her rope' with me by mid-afternoon. With no concept of how to play or be a child with me she tried to make me an adult. The more I tried to get things right the more I aggravated her. When she had enough of me she would put me behind the door in the lounge room. There was about a foot and a half of wall on one side so that I had a small triangle of space. It was an effective way to silence me as my sniffing tears or scuffling brought down more wrath and threats that the forthcoming punishment would be harsher. For a child with an active mind and body this was close to hell, but this was merely the holding cell; for the real punishment lay ahead. Punishment that was Dad's duty to inflict. Knowing this was ahead, I was not merely bored, but anxious and fearful. I began to chew my tongue and this became a lifetime habit.

She would leave me there for hours, tense unbearable hours. Then I would hear Dad's whistle as he came down the concrete path at the side of the house. As he arrived at the back door my confinement was over as Mum dragged me out by the arm, head down and trembling, to be handed to Dad, along with a long lists of my faults and failures. His shoulders would slump and his eyes cloud over as he got the strap from its hanging place in the wardrobe and delivered the stinging stripes at Mum's command. Many were the times when she told him to hit me again. I found it impossible to blame him, as his eyes were often filled with tears, as if he hated this task of fatherhood, whereas Mum's eyes would shine with satisfaction that some unfathomable score had been settled. I know my brother suffered the same fate as we would try to hide the strap together and he would try to hide me and protect me. I remember once when he hid me at the bottom of his cupboard and begged Mum to let him take my belting. And that, more than chasing snakes, made him my hero.

However, my biggest fear by far was that if I made mistakes, my mother's love would be withdrawn; lost. So I didn't fear punishment as much as the inherent rejection that accompanied it. Sometimes she would banish me angrily to my room for hours. I would watch her from the window of my room while I was in exile wondering why I was such a failure at tidiness, order and pleasing my mother.

I remember her stiffened back as she pegged the clothes on the line with increased purpose while her anger towards me slowly cooled. If I live to be one hundred I will never forget the look of her back. Her face may blur and soften with time and with forgetting but not that stiffened back. It will forever remain a symbol of her turning away from me and my helplessness to bridge the gap between us. I had early assumed the role of making her happy, making her life smooth. I tried to live in the narrow confines of the world that she made for me, but it was her world. The rules and punishments meted out confused me. I felt a crushing sense of failure.

As a child you have no reference point for these things, every home is just like your home. There are no other realities. You whisper to small friends about 'smacks' and suchlike and you believe what grownups or parents tell you—that you must suffer physical pain in order to learn to be good. There were days when I had rows of black bruising that made it to painful to sit properly and I tugged constantly at the hem of my uniform in case the marks would be seen and my shame revealed. In my childish mind those marks were proof of my wrongdoing. The world would know that I must have been very bad to cause such punishment. It never occurred to me to think that anyone would see them as wrong being done to me. I don't think any child in that situation thinks that way unless they are told or shown differently.

I later learned that such punishments had nothing to do with making anyone good. I learned that the shame I felt about making my mother angry didn't belong to me. I had earned no shame. My perceptions were distorted.

I suffered the most terrifying nightmares and wasn't allowed any light to comfort me, just a quick few words, 'be quiet now and think of heaven'. Many times my very presence seemed to aggravate her. I overheard her talking to a neighbour with an incredulous tone.

'She is never still, she is never quiet, she can never keep track of her things—she would lose her head if it wasn't screwed on.'

Perhaps I rejected my mother's time-consuming routines because I perceived them as very real competitors in my attempt to gain her love and attention. I remember her working long into the night, utterly exhausted, ironing towels or rearranging cupboards.

I remember a time when punishment was meted out to me and I was justly ashamed of myself. I had seen a small friend throw a particularly spectacular tantrum and being given an ice cream when our family was out on a day trip on a ferry. Being a bit of a performer I followed her routine to a T. I was quite proud of my first tantrum until one swift slice of Dad's hand had me sitting on my bottom on the deck.

'Just in case you are wondering, Linda. That means no ice cream as well.'

I remember that I looked up at him in awe. He had quietly and firmly put me in my place and showed me the limits of bad behaviour. I had received precisely what I had deserved. I remember thinking, I asked for that. When I stood up and rubbed my rear end I reached out and held his hand and he held mine.

Dad came to realise that in my contented hours with him in the shed I committed none of the crimes assigned to me by Mum and he refused to mete out any further beltings. When I began to menstruate he made one simple statement that meant my freedom from the fear of physical reprisal.

'No-one will ever hit my daughter again.' I remember his steely eyes, his soft words and quiet determination. He looked at me; sorrow and forgiveness passed silently between us.

Tiptoe while shouting

'Oh my God, you too. It happened to you too.'

The words came tumbling out of my school friend's mouth in the middle of what had started as an average, polite conversation, catching up.

My mind went blank, thoughts whirled through my head, whirring and making me dizzy. Feeling faint, I fought the compulsion to put my head down. Don't think. Don't think. Think. Think. 'Beth' and I had just been talking about the town we grew up in, my tenth birthday party and some of the people we knew from school and the dusty country streets.

She had mentioned the name of a man who lived near our family. A man I had visited as a child. A softly spoken attentive man. A man who liked children.

'Come and visit me anytime,' he had said. 'I like little girls. I have a wonderful swing. You will love it.'

I had described the house he and his family lived in, in vivid detail. The layout of the house, the kitchen window that faced north where the sun blazed in through pure white shimmering chiffon. The window sill behind those gently fluttering curtains held a huge round container of lollies of all colours, shapes and sizes. The back room that I had never discerned whether it was bedroom or office. I'd told her the colour of the chenille bedspread, the tidy desk, pristine surfaces and a bookshelf with all the books methodically placed according to size. It had fascinated me, that order, that meticulous arrangement.

'Beth' stood before me with her hand on my arm as I struggled to take it in. And then she told me what he had done to her. I felt ill and faint again.

'No! No! That didn't happen to me,' I remonstrated, my mind spinning.

Beth pulled me into the nearest coffee shop, gently leading me by the arm to the farthest table from the busy shopping throng.

My heart was sinking and I was drowning, knowing, but not wanting to know, the truth I had denied for decades.

'Think about it Linda. Do you ever remember any other house in such detail? Even houses you have lived in?'

I swallowed a lump the size of a melon. Oh God, so it *was* true. The nightmare real. No. No.

'No. I can't remember any house like that house. But maybe I imagined what the house was like, dreamed it,' I said, struggling for traction in my head. 'And I don't remember anything happening, anything like what happened to you.'

'What do you remember?'

'Well it was very ordinary really, just a visit. I ...well he had a swing out the back, not a tyre swing like near the creek, but one with a bench seat like the parks. We would sit inside in the kitchen for a while and he would offer me one of those lollies...' I fell silent.

'From the huge jar on the window sill, with every kind of lolly,' Beth added softly.

'Yes. I took one. I took it to be polite. Mum always said it was rude to refuse, unless it was a stranger. He wasn't a stranger. I didn't want to take one because I hated lollies, still do, and many sweets for that matter. The only lollies I liked were Jaffas™.'

'Well chocolate is the sixth food group,' Beth said smiling.

I was feeling nauseated. Seeing my pale face Beth hailed a passing waitress and ordered a cup of tea. She paused, not wanting to lead, but allowing me to take my time. I knew she didn't want to place thoughts into my head; false memories.

'Then he'd ask me if I would like to have a swing and I would say, 'Yes, please. I love swings', and he would push the swing for hours. Well it felt like hours. I would float and wonder if I was moving or if I was standing still and the world around me moving. The next thing I would remember was being in the back room on the bed with the red chenille bedspread.'

Beth sipped her tea. I remembered the cup in front of me and starting sipping the warm sweet brew.

'Do you remember going into the back room?' Beth asked.

'No. I would tell him I felt funny. 'I'm never sick, and I'm never sleepy—why Mum says I never sit still long enough to rest,' I would tell him. And he would say, 'Never mind.' Then I would ask why there was a bed in the office, who slept there and where was Mrs Eildon, and he would softly say, 'Never mind about any of those things,' so I stopped asking. It had been so ingrained in us children that it was rude to pry in other people's lives. She said I asked more questions than there would ever be answers for.'

I would hang my head.

'I'm sorry for asking questions. Mum says it's rude.'

'It's alright,' he would say softly.

'Did you talk about it?' asked Beth.

'I wouldn't have known what to say. I didn't know what had happened, except that I felt tired and sick, disorientated really. You can't articulate that as a child. It sounds like nothing. I liked the swing and he was kind.'

'But it wasn't nothing.'

'No, it wasn't nothing. It has haunted me; the wondering. My lips were silent but my mind was screaming. It was like going through life, tiptoeing while shouting. I had nightmares every night. Nightmares of running until my legs had no power, then crawling until my knees gave way and then grabbing at the grass to help pull me along; away. Away from a faceless man.'

'You don't have to tiptoe anymore.'

'That's good because I was crap at it anyway. but I can still scream surely?'

'Absolutely darling, if you must, but just not here, not now!'

'I have too much respect for your ears. And there is always the fact that I've never been thrown out of an eatery and don't intend to start now.'

'You have my eternal gratitude,' Beth said, laughing. Then she become serious again. 'It doesn't go away if you deny it, compress it or trivialise it.'

'Don't I know it! If there is ever a news article, a television show, or even a conversation about sexual abuse I begin to sweat, my heart races and I have to leave the room feeling ill. I never reacted quite as strongly when there were images of preemie babies, and they reminded me of David, the baby who died of cot death.'

Beth took a pen out of her purse and wrote the name of the counsellor for the local women's refuge on a serviette.

'She's brilliant. No waffle, no wallowing or digging in the past; just moving forward

'I need to see that house.'

'No time like the present.'

Beth drove me past the house and it was exactly as I imagined. It was an image that had been branded into my mind. It wasn't a dream. I made an appointment with the counsellor.

Just as Beth had promised, Kate was brilliant.

'What is the thought that comes into your mind when you think about who you are?'

'What's wrong with me? But doesn't everyone think that?'

'No,' Kate said smiling. 'It may surprise you to know that many people don't think that in a lifetime, much less whenever they are faced with who they are.'

'But I don't remember everything, just the unease, the nausea and sleeping.'

'The heart and soul always remember what the mind denies. It's how we protect ourselves when we are powerless and vulnerable as children.'

Just as Beth had predicted, Kate led me gently into my future. A future that wasn't founded on the past. We spent no time on why, or what or how. There was no focus on the motives or actions of the man.

'Some people need to confront the person and some don't.'

'Bit hard to confront a tombstone,' I quipped and Kate smiled. 'But no, I wouldn't want to confront him.'

'That's okay. It's about you changing you, opening the door to healing. Learning to love the person that you are. Finding the truth of your own worth. His agenda doesn't matter here, but I can tell you that you weren't the only one with this man.'

'Oh,' I whispered, shaken by the confirmation. He was indeed a predator.

For the first time in my life I kept a journal. Not a record of daily meanderings of the mind, the fickle highs and lows of mood. A gratitude journal; of daily victories, warm responses from others— marked recorded. A journal of goals, of clarity of purpose. A life plan. As the journal unfolded my life gained momentum. The pleasures of life, the affirmation from others was there in black and white. Real, authentic and lasting.

I had learned the invaluable truth that acknowledging wasn't 'making too much of things', but that it was cutting it down to size, making less of it. And coincidentally taking the power from the experience and giving it back to me.

When I felt strong enough I shared it with Mum. She had already reached out and listened to how I felt about her stern mothering.

'I never knew you felt that way. I never intended to hurt you.' Tears welled in her eyes and she swallowed hard at the story.

'I would have killed him,' she said, her eyes fierce with protecting love. I wondered afresh if I should have told her, or left her in ignorance.

'Thank you for telling me. It helps me understand you and explains some of your reactions. It has made a little sense of how you acted and the fearfulness you sometimes showed. Yes, it's a good thing you told me. After all, you're not just my daughter; you've become my best friend.'

A launch pad and a ragged purse

I have always believed that all of your life that has gone before prepares you for where you are now. I remember not long after I met my second husband, Adam and I was studying for my Diploma in Nursing Administration by external studies through Armidale, UNE. I had my final exams to sit and he had a desperate need to discuss some heavy emotional issues that were impacting on him the night before my last exam. I got no study done and had very little sleep either. I drove to Harristown and sat the exams.

The exam consisted of writing two comprehensive case studies of palliative care patients. As I had nursed both my father and my mother's sister just prior to their deaths I found it relatively easy to write about them and their daily care and needs as I had attended to all their care for many years.

Adam expressed some bumbling comments that sounded like remorse when he apologised for keeping me from studying. His regret didn't last long when I told him that the exam had been "a breeze". Then I received the 'people like you don't deserve success in life, things just come too easy to you don't they!' I told him that I had been preparing to sit that exam for many heartbreaking years of experience. Converse to what he thought I had indeed done a great deal of preparation for that exam. A great deal of living life.

No-one has come from a vacuum. Sometimes we are gifted habits that cripple us in life.

I once had a dementia patient in one of the nursing homes I worked at who refused to eat after she arrived at the nursing home. She had been living in home and surviving precariously. She was obsessed with the fact that she had no money to pay for her meals. No one could get her to even sit at the table. She was living in the fog of dementia and felt that she had to earn her keep. I went and sat with her in an armchair in the patients' lounge. I asked about her day. I became her friend. An old dear friend. We talked of shopping and the fun we had. Of the years. Of the tears. I asked if she was hungry. She was a 'mite peckish'. So was I. How about lunch then? I ventured. But I have no money; she said with sunken shoulders and showed me the ragged inside of her empty purse. That's Ok, I said, I have already paid for us, you have been such a dear friend to me so come and have lunch, it's all paid for and ready. She came; she was no longer a stranger but the guest of a friend. She didn't get the purse out again at mealtime. The pattern had been broken. She was home.

So often in life we allow our imaginary limitations make us refuse the gracious gifts of life and love because we have based our own worth on what we believe is our own ragged contribution. Every moment we live is a preparation or a rehearsal for the next moment.

Sometimes we don't choose the ragged purse we have been given in life, but we can learn to choose to accept the grace and love of others. We can change, we can do things differently. I came to motherhood with a ragged purse, an empty space, a hungry childhood. A place of fear that had been ruled by the constrictions and harshness of a mother trapped in her own alien world. She knew no other way, no other love. Fear was the 'Houston', the rocket pad from which I was launched. It was the story that built my realities and created my fantasies. It was chaos, confusion but mostly fear. Fear, like the hounds of the Baskervilles always inches from your ankles. Snapping, snarling and threatening. Fear because you don't understand. Fear because you can't ask questions. And fear of getting it all wrong.

Sometimes she would banish me to my room. I would watch her from the window of my room while I was in exile wondering why I was such a failure at tidiness, order and pleasing my mother. I remember her stiffened back as she pegged the clothes on the line with increased purpose while her anger towards me slowly cooled. If I live to be one hundred I will never forget the look of her back. Her face may blur and soften with time and with forgetting but not that stiffened back. It will forever remain a symbol of her turning away from me and my helplessness to bridge the gap between us. I had early assumed the role of making her happy, making her life smooth. I tried to live in the narrow confines of the world that she made for me. Her world. Her rules and the punishments meted out confused me. I felt a crushing sense of failure.

I suffered terrifying nightmares and not allowed any light to comfort me, with just a quick word from her of 'be quiet now and think of heaven'. Many times my very presence seemed to aggravate her, I heard her tell the neighbours with a sharp edge to her voice, 'she is never still, she is never quiet, she can never keep track of her things—she would lose her head if it wasn't screwed on'. I was seldom allowed to play inside the immaculate house with this list of defects and misdemeanours under my belt. It seemed there was an unwritten rule that indoors was for those who kept things orderly. And children, she found, were very lacking in this regard.

I understand these things better now but as a child you have no reference point for these things. In the mind of the child every home is just like your home. There are no other realities. You whisper to small friends about 'smacks' and suchlike and you believe what the grownups or parents tell you. That you must suffer physical pain in order to learn to be good. I later learned that such punishments had nothing to do with making anyone good. I learned that the shame I felt about making my mother angry didn't belong to me. I had earned no shame. My perceptions of love and parenthood were distorted. After my disastrous attempts at marriage I began to feel that perhaps my past childhood experiences were colouring my world and as fast as I had tried to outrun them, they were gaining on me and in fact had never left at all. It slowly, reluctantly began to dawn on me that I had chosen men who would take over where my mother had left off. It was beginning to feel very much as if my childhood was being repeated, revisited.

After all this is not such a strange phenomenon. Why if we were raised speaking Spanish then it would be perfectly natural to respond every time we heard someone speak Spanish. It would resonate deep within and we would be drawn instinctively to someone who spoke the language we are familiar with. Why should it be any different with our emotional landscape? We wonder why we are attracted to people later in life when it really is simple that we have heard a timeless lyric that is deep in our psyche. We may not know why but we respond erringly like a compass to magnetic north. We sense home.

I can't find my son!

Not long after returning to Warrigal I attempted to rediscover 'me time'. Of course, it ended in disaster. With Bronson on access menacing his father I attempted to reintroduce myself to a social life. Starting out in a small way I arranged to go to the movies with a friend and Luke. I thought I would relax but soon discovered that I was unable to leave behind crisis mode. On a casual night out at the movies only thirty kilometres from home my panic reflex kicked in. I lost Luke.

Every parent knows the sinking, ghastly, feeling that assails you when you think that your child has gone missing. Some parents phone hospitals, some arrange funerals in their minds. As children when my brother and I arrived home my mother would invariably say, 'We were just on our way to ring the Police!' My mother was the spokesperson for We. They had apparently been from anxiety to anger and back again several times without taking the car out of the garage.

On this night my friend Lynette, my son Luke and I met up with another carload of friends at the movie theatre. I was suffering PDDS (Post-Divorce Distress Syndrome). I was feeling a little precarious emotionally and behaving over protectively, oh alright, downright clingy. As I had to drive home a long way after the movies I had impressed on my thoughtful, malleable son that he must come along with me and drive us home again afterwards. I hadn't been out for ages and had lost a lot of confidence.

The movie was great, the night was great, and then it was time to go home. When we came out of the movies it was pitch black. I had been in another world for the past few hours and was disoriented by the darkness. I struggled to get my bearings. We all left to go to the cars. We didn't all get there. I had seen my short-sighted son go down the stairs into the parking lot but he didn't arrive at the car. I quickly decided that some unseen force had taken him. The same unseen force pushed me over the edge between rationality and insanity. It was a rough ride, the destination as inevitable as night following day.

I wandered the whole car park, moaning and wailing like a professional mourner, until there were no cars left. Lynnette, a tall cool blonde woman, was completely fazed by my abandonment of the professional nurse for the guise of madwoman. She had never seen me like this, and after a brief attempt to rein me in, realised I was driving this train wreck and nothing was going to stop me. My distress finally got the attention of the security guard with my plaintive, 'I can't find my son'. A lean man with a compassionate face he saw at once the seriousness of the situation or more likely was perplexed by such raw emotion, and promptly phoned the Police. A burly officer with a thick blonde moustache attended the call and proceeded to sort out the dilemma. In true investigative style he began to question me.

'What is wrong, Madam.'

'I can't find my son.'

'How old is your son Madam?'

'Seventeen.'

'And how tall is he?' At this particular point a very small light came on in my brain. I ignored it and went for broke. I became a little vague.

'Oh, he's around 6 foot, I guess.'

'You mean to tell me that you have called me out to look for a seventeen year old boy who is about 6 foot tall! What do you expect me to do?' No sympathy here.

'Well,' said I, annoyed more by his attitude than the realities at this point, 'Well, pardon me officer I haven't been watching the news, I didn't realise that people of a certain age and size were exempt from being attacked, cut up in pieces and thrown over the fence. I don't know what you should do I'm sure, I am his mother and I'm supposed to panic and I am panicking, you must have gone to Police school to learn what to do in this kind of situation.'

At that, the officer got an unusual glint in his eye. I wondered if they had a code for 'I've got a live one'. Any minute now he would put an all-points bulletin nutcase alert. He must have decided to take valour over discretion. Smarter than me.

'Well I can't do anything here; we'll have to go to the station.'

Not knowing to leave well enough alone I ploughed on, digging my own grave deeper by the minute.

'You mean to tell me that every 12 year old on the North Shore has a mobile phone and the Government can't even supply the police force with walkie talkie thingy's'. An attempt to confound him with technical jargon failed as I forgot what to call them. He judiciously ignored this remark and told me to follow him to the station.

What followed can only be described as a high speed police chase with all the road rules ignored. The only difference was that in this case the suspect was trying to keep up with the Police. After weaving around in lanes all over Earlston we arrived at a squat dark building with one small flickering light vainly trying to dispel the darkness. At this stage all pretence at manners eluded him and the officer disappeared into the building leaving me in the parking lot. I was obviously at the back of the station and I was furious. Emboldened by my new sense of injustice I called out at the first available doorway, 'Am I supposed to follow you or have you gone to the John?' This brave, rather loud statement was not met with silence but by the guffaws of his fellow officers who sensed some free entertainment. The officer returned to the parking lot to show me in. I didn't know policemen could blush.

When I arrived in the interview room the place was packed with smiling policemen. The reluctance the sneering moustachioed officer had towards dealing with me had evidently been replaced with a sincere desire to help me on my way with all possible speed. We had met some people at the movies and they were known to my friend Lynette. She told the officer their names and he phoned them. Of course they had all arrived home by this time, along with my son, and had even caught a little sleep. So simple. Common sense told me that I possibly owed the officer an apology. Common sense did not prevail. Falsely assuming that things couldn't get any worse the officer decided to show his magnanimous nature and invited me for coffee 'sometime'. This innocuous suggestion I refused out of hand. I was strangely reluctant to let go of the wronged and misunderstood citizen role. I was not to be placated. I very politely informed him just what he could do with his coffee.

I then decided on a suitably dramatic exit, thanked the officers, expressed concern for the rest of the night's entertainment and their danger of imminent boredom, wished them well, headed towards the dark doorway that appeared to be the exit, said goodnight and walked straight into the cells.

'Shit!' I said.

An 'aha' moment

'I killed my father's rabbit and broke his heart,' I confided to my oldest son, Gerard, as he put new brake pads on my front brakes. We were standing near his rabbit hutch.

We'd been chatting about general things and as soon as the words were out of my mouth I wanted to take them back, desperately. When would I learn to choose the right moment? But then again, there never seemed a right moment for so many things I said, so I just sighed and hoped he hadn't heard.

'You did what?' Gerard asked, putting down tool he'd been holding.

I looked over at his pet rabbit Flopsy, the one with the permanently bent ear that scared the crap out of the neighbourhood cats. I'd been staring at Flopsy for five minutes with the warm sun on my back and floating back into the past.

'I killed my father's rabbit and broke his heart,' I repeated. I was sunk anyway. 'It was my job to put the hessian bags over his hutch every night to keep him warm in winter. I was so sure I had done it, but when I got up in the morning there was a huge fuss in the kitchen. Dad was upset, my brother Peter was looking like a bomb hit him and Mum was holding forth like a warlord. She looked furiously at me when I came into the room, then pointed at me.'

'There's the culprit,' she said accusingly. 'It's her job to cover the hutch.'

The rest became a blur as I heard ... frozen stiff ... poor thing ... didn't have a chance ... never trust Linda with anything...'

I was a criminal and like all good criminals before me, I went on the run. Having little imagination and resources at seven years of age I went to hide behind the dunny only to find Dad there weeping for his lost pet. Benny the rabbit, used to jump into Dad's lap and hop around him. His heart was broken and it was my fault. I'd murdered his pet and broken his heart.

My son looked gobsmacked. I waited for his condemnation, hanging my head.

'For God's sake mum, how could you believe that rubbish! Have you ever told anyone this?'

'Of course not stupid, who confesses to murder!'

He looked at me and was grinning broadly.

'Silly little mother, rabbits come from England. They live *in the snow*. The bloody rabbit died in the night of natural causes and was stiff with rigor mortis.'

'So you don't put bags on Flopsy's hutch?'

'God no, hessian bags on a hutch wouldn't keep the cold out anyway. He has been outside through three winters! We come out in the morning and he is happily nibbling grass with ice on his whiskers. Geez, poor silly mother.'

'So I don't need to knit Flopsy a jumper,' I said, fighting back tears.

He came purposefully around the car and held me in his arms.

'You daft woman! You didn't kill your father's rabbit and you never broke his heart.'

A man called Ray

In my travels around the neighbourhood I had visited Ray, our neighbourhood 'eccentric'. Yes, even more than me! He is the one whose birds had been kept awake at night with my sensor setting security lights off every time Diane's cat walked past. His colourful obscenities peppered his speech and if you ever interrupted him he would say, 'Will you ever shut up, you bitch, I am trying to talk to you!'

I found him immensely kind and knew that when he called me bitch I was being given the ultimate term of endearment. For in spite of his language he is the gentlest and most caring man alive, who is known to water gardens, care for pets, carry groceries and help anyone. Just before I arrived there he had been helping the sweet old painter whose body was ravaged by cancer one door up from him to load his things to take to the retirement village. With his ragged appearance and the perpetual fag hanging out of his mouth he was a complete shock to the local clergyman who arrived to collect the cheque for the retirement home. 'Don't worry mate, I'm not thievin', I'm just helpin' the old guy out'. This straightforward approach was an even bigger shock to the impeccably dressed, stunned pastor. It was just as well that Ray didn't get around to his usual language antics and say something the poor pastor could never repeat to a living soul.

What a surprise is in store for that pastor when he gets to the pearly gates and finds Ray standing there next to St Peter saying 'Come in mate, hurry up, you're creatin' a breeze through the open door standin' there gapin' like a chimpanzee'. Ray himself will be shocked to find himself in a heaven he could not conceive after leaving a world that to him had no God of love that he could ever believe in although he has spent his life with the rarest kind of generosity of spirit. When you look within. There is beauty everywhere. If you look. It comes from the place of believing in true equality. Not the kind of sitting in church and looking at those supposedly above you and saying I am as good as them. But looking at everyone apparently below you and seeing within. Try it sometime. You are in for the shock of your life.

So when I arrived I was greeted with, 'Go 'round the back, ya silly bitch, ya can't get in the front door.' We had a very congenial cup of tea and a chat with only the occasional, 'Will you for Christ's sake, shut up'. The phone rang and he greeted the caller with, 'How are you, ya sexual maniac,' this was apparently a devoted and favourite nephew enquiring after his health because he had undergone recent exhaustive medical tests. 'Oh no mate, I'm fucked,' he said. 'No seriously, I'm dying mate, yeah, got the cancer every which way 'til Sunday, no I can't have the chemotherapy or the radiotherapy because of the open-heart surgery, but I won't be hitting the downhill slope until November. Don't let it worry you mate, I will be around for a while yet, Christ doesn't want me and the Devil is booked solid'.

After this cheerful exchange he sat down and resumed his chat with me without losing a single thread of our conversation, quite possibly leaving a devastated nephew on the end of the phone line. Or perhaps the nephew knew this marvellous man and his incredible attitude to life well. I told him about my escapades with bullies, vandals and thieves and went off home with Ray sending his fond regards to Bronson who he regarded as a 'beaut little guy' with lovely manners and told me to tell Bronson to come to him any time he was worried. The worst bully lived opposite Ray in the street parallel to me. Ray started looking out for Bronson.

After a week or so Ray rang me with his usual 'getting straight to the point' attitude. 'What 'ave you been up to ya bloody bitch there hasn't been a kid in the street for the last week? Only a few really little tikes who seem really confused that they have the street to themselves and are making the most of it without the big bullies messin' with 'em and the main culprit hasn't come out of the back yard kickin' a football, and I never seen that kid look at a football before!' I could only reply that I guessed the local Police must have sorted them and wondered how soon I should leave town before the reprisal from those whom the Yugoslavian neighbour had intensely intoned to me 'They hatea you'.

From there I went to insure my house and contents and although I truly attempted to have a serious conversation explaining my need for insurance due to imminent threat of neighbourhood terrorism I managed to have the NRMA girl putting her hand over her mouth and apologizing with great mirth for finding my desperate situation hilarious. She was even more amused when she asked the value of my furniture and I said I had obtained most of it from St Vincent's and seconds shops and recovered it and restored it. Instead of admiring my collecting of eclectic antiquities she merely began to laugh harder.

Pedant

Some people can only see one point-of-view so they come across as thinking themselves superior to the rest of us. They don't have the ability to walk a mile in any other shoes and this makes them sound pedantic. This is because they are pedantic. They make good headmasters. I know this because I married one. A pedant and a headmaster. Adam was never wrong. Lesser mortals were referred to as 'you people'. 'You people' didn't know what they were talking about. 'You people' couldn't see something right in front of their eyes. I can remember listening in awe to his many finely delivered lectures. I must have driven him nuts. When he was in full flight I would often interrupt and say, 'don't let the facts interfere with a good story'. And he was good. With his towering height and his sportsman's physique he was impressive, before he spoke that is. He had such an air of confident authority and such a booming voice that many people would have believed him if he said he and not Moses had led the children of Israel across the Red Sea. I tried not to question or argue with him in public. I didn't try hard enough.

When we lived in Crofton Park Adam was the headmaster of a two teacher school. The school was comprised of two long white buildings with several classrooms in each building. The buildings were at right angles to each other and a concrete meeting area lay between them. Both buildings were lined with windows and all the rooms were filled with light and colour. Many colourful crafts and paintings displaying childish artistry adorned the walls. This was a community school with a lovely family atmosphere. An elderly gardener, who had been a nurseryman, lovingly tended the lawns and a circular garden filled with petunias, Shasta daisies and alyssum grew in proliferation near the school gates. There was a lush green playing field just beneath a grassy hill that we used one year as a water slide with the adults screaming down the incline along with the children. And beyond that was the ever present red clay soil, which was jokingly referred to by the locals as making all the men taller by adding layers of thick mud to their boots.

Every year the school held a combined schools' sports day for the kids. One year, before the event a group of mothers approached Adam to ask him why the children weren't practicing for the sports day when it was only three weeks away. He informed them in haughty, offended tones that it was impossible to do so when he hadn't been given the list of events that would be held. How could he prepare when he was in the dark about the very relevant details necessary to prepare the children? It was a command performance and I would have let it rest if he hadn't been particularly condescending to me a few days before. When he turned to me for support, with the victory smile on his face adding 'isn't that right, Linda!' I upset the applecart completely by saying that he had outdone himself and that was the biggest load of rubbish I had heard for some time. 'They have the same events every year and have had since I was going to school. Had this changed? I don't think so. Do they have pole vaulting for six year olds? I don't think so. Anyway whatever events are on the agenda would involve running very fast or throwing balls, it doesn't take rocket science to work that out. They could practice that couldn't they?' As I said I probably drove him nuts.

Whenever we travelled if Adam needed to stop at the service station to use the bathroom he insisted that *everyone* go. He would wake everyone up and demand that we all got out and went to the toilet. This did not go down well with the teenagers in the car. Or with me. I would salute him or dance on the spot and call him Daddy. *This* did not go down well with Adam.

Once Adam had a three day argument with Luke about Nebuchadnezzar, the Persian King in the Old Testament who lived like an animal and survived for nine years by eating grass. Luke suggested that it was not possible for a human being to do this and that the lesson the Bible was trying to teach had nothing to do with the ingestion of plant cellulose. Luke's opinion was not welcome, and Adam proceeded to tell him at great length how wrong he was. As usual this involved long and pedantic searches through the encyclopedia and any other resource that either of them saw fit to come up with. Luke was highly amused and entertained with this diversion from all the other boredoms of life and entered into it with some zeal. Adam was not at all amused *or* entertained but also entered into it with an altogether different zeal. I went to bed. The debate was long and intellectual. Adam ended with his favourite statement, 'I know I'm right', and Luke fell back on his usual ploy and said nothing, that is until he remarked much later, 'he's an idiot'. The idiot could thereafter be goaded on this subject at the drop of a hat.

Tristan

I once knew a boy named Tristan. He was the four year old son of a big square competent guy that I dated between marriages. He was the kind of boy the writer of 'Ginger Meggs' had in mind. A surer candidate for ADHD could not have been found. With wispy fine blonde hair curling out at all angles he looked like a wild angel. His beguiling blue eyes were huge and constantly full to the brim with surprise. He was a traffic stopper. *Literally.* If horns blared in the street you could bet a King's ransom Tristan was in the street, stopping traffic.

His father had his own unique style of reality therapy for this kind of behaviour. After said incident he would take Tristan out the back of the house and tell him in the strongest terms that his life would be cut short, he would never live to play with his toys again, and he would be dead and buried in a hole with the dirt banged on top. The boy's eyes would grow as large as saucers. All would be well until the fire brigade came down the street. A good five minutes later. Horns blared. Back to the drawing board. Or in this case the backyard to demonstrate a hole with the dirt banged on top. The frequency of this behaviour smacked strongly of the point not being taken.

Luke was eight at the time and he had a dog named Monty. This erratic, lovable mutt, a cross between a German Shepherd and a Husky, had been named by his previous owners because of his love for Monte Carlo biscuits. The dog's frenetic curling tail was at comical variance to his dark intense face. We strongly suspected that Monty had been given marijuana which was a part of the previous owner's staple 'diet'.

Tristan also had a dog, or more correctly, his father did. Cindy was an ex-police dog who was as well behaved as the boy was not. She seemed to experience great embarrassment on finding herself in the many precarious situations Tristan placed her in. Her eyebrows would be twitching and her noble face with awash with apology. She would stand obediently at attention while Tristan lifted her tail and tried to insert a stick. After all the discipline of being a police dog it must have been extremely trying to find herself with a four year old who would have given Attila the Hun a run for his money.

One day Tristan decided he would talk to the rabbit that was on loan from the school. It was

Luke's privilege to have the class pet for a weekend. Soon the cry went out from the neighbours that the rabbit was on the loose. Cindy lay down and cried. Monty took chase and cornered the rabbit three doors down with Luke in hot pursuit and the rest of us following. Monty, who had eaten all of our chicks soon after they hatched, seemed for some reason, strangely reluctant to sink his teeth into the rabbit. The rabbit was rescued and returned to the hutch with its heart racing. On questioning Tristan, the four year old, informed us that he 'didn't leck the rabbit out, it lecked itself out.'

Not content with this feat Tristan decided to follow this gag up by putting both dogs in the chicken coup that housed Luke's adult hens and two grossly proud Rhode Island Red roosters. Cindy retreated to the corner of the coup and put her paws over her eyes. Monty pursued the colourful roosters round the enclosure and by the time we arrived they were missing their tail feathers and much of their pride. Both roosters refused to come out of the coup until their feathers had re-grown.

Tristan was punished by having to lie on a bed for half an hour's time out. During this time he managed to sneak into the kitchen and polish off an entire packet of Kingston creams. This time, however, he was unable to blame anyone else, as he was covered in biscuit crumbs.

Tristan had two very sweet Nanas. Tristan didn't swear. He made up for this character defect by telling people to 'ping off'. He once tried this neat trick on Luke's stocky no-nonsense Nan, my mother. Wrong move. Little Red Riding Hood would have been relieved to find the wolf in this granny's bed. You get the picture. There was no quiet lecture on manners. That day I think he got the true meaning of what it was to 'ping off'.

Courthouse blues

Adam's anger continued after we moved to Warrigal and I was fearful. I went trembling with the church pastor to get my first AVO. Adam always adjourned the hearings. By about the third time I got a little braver.

I was at the local courthouse one hot Tuesday in the middle of an Australian heat wave. My new legal aid solicitor seemed to be very impressed with this marvellous specimen with his shiny shoes and polite manner. She took one look at him and expressed that I would never get what I wanted against 'that man'. I decided I would represent myself so I came dressed for the part. I wore a fitted navy suit that I had made, white silk cowl-neck blouse, navy stockings and high heels. I wore my hair up and had make up on. I carried a black briefcase that anyone would have been surprised to discover held my shopping list. I arrived early.

When I walked past the crowd waiting outside with their peasant tops, checked flannelette shirts and thongs and went inside to the toilets before the others I was delighted to hear someone say, 'The solicitors have started to arrive'. I was relieved that at least I looked like I was up to the job but the truth was that I was terrified. I had come alone. I would face the magistrate and I had no idea what to call him or what to say but I consoled myself with the fact that the only thing required of me would be to tell the truth humbly.

Just before our case was to be heard there was a beautiful, bruised and tearful woman asking through her solicitor for an AVO on her ex who was brought into the court in handcuffs, scruffy and defiant. When the magistrate saw her reluctance to allow this 'detainee' to collect his things from the home they had shared he was tough on this delicate, tearful creature and said the police had better things to do than help collect belongings when people couldn't work out their own lives. This caused more delicate weeping on the part of the delicate creature with the tiny girl clinging to her mother's skirts and also had the effect on the moron in the dock to feel emboldened to assume that he was now the wronged party. This was a crucial mistake. The magistrate turned on him and said, 'You are the one in the dock in handcuffs here and you are going back downstairs to the cell shortly, don't get any ideas about yourself!' The moron hung his head and the magistrate swiftly determined that the woman could organise one of her family to be present when the moron came to collect his things. The gavel banged.

I swallowed—hard. Adam and I were up next. This magistrate was going to eat me. Here I was with the gall to eschew legal representation. How could I tell the magistrate that I felt I didn't stand a chance of winning with a legal aid solicitor who showed all the usual signs of actually fancying my ex-husband? The magistrate called our case and Adam's solicitor stood so I followed suit. He had a few words to the Adam's solicitor and then quietly asked if I was representing myself.

'Yes, your honour'. He thankfully did not question my sanity on this decision which was truly soothing as I was doing enough of that myself.

'Mr Dixon requests that there be an adjournment of three weeks, your honour' postulated the haughty man who represented my ex-husband.

'Do you wish to oppose this, Mrs Dixon?' politely enquired the magistrate.

'Well, your honour, does Mr Dixon have the right to postpone the hearing?' I politely enquired of the magistrate.

'Yes, he does, Mrs Dixon'.

'Well then, your honour, I see no point in objecting'.

The gavel banged. Hearing set down for the blah blah. What a nice man I thought, feeling quite the opposite of being eaten. After a few more adjournments Adam couldn't resist getting up and interjecting. This did not go down well with the magistrate who pointed out that Adam had paid good money for someone else to represent him. So the gavel was banged in my favour with very few words from me and the absence of any legal strategy whatever.

In my usual irrepressible style I actually began to enjoy these outings to the court for AVO's. Safely seated on the court benches outside waiting to be called I engaged in one of my favourite pastimes of people watching and observing. I was amazed when one mother lifted her child by the arm and thoroughly whacked its bum in full view of the court office and the rest of us who would soon be the gallery, plus a couple of relaxed policemen. Ye gods, what a place this was!

By the fourth time I was getting a bit bored so started to strike up conversations with complete strangers. As I do. Sitting outside courts I found brought out the strange propensity for people to talk to themselves. Having had the cheek of the devil as a child I had always assumed that this was an invitation for anyone present to join in. One day when I was sitting there I was next to a well dressed dark haired man of Mediterranean descent who kept repeating to himself, 'I don't know why I'm here?' At first I answered him silently in my head with the thought, 'Hello it is Tuesday, the day put aside for domestic violence or the occasional murder—and those boys are usually wearing handcuffs and have personal escorts.'

After he repeated this several times I felt compelled to explain life to him. I started innocently enough—a sign my friends would have recognized as trouble but not him, 'So, you don't understand?' This seemingly sympathetic remark had the effect of loosening his tongue considerably. He didn't seem to notice that he was surrounded by quite a few other people engaged in fear, boredom, apprehensive chain smoking and there was a woman on the other side of me who was enthusiastically wailing her way through large box of tissues that her friend held helplessly in front of her.

'I thought we were happy, I thought we had a great marriage, twenty years together and I never saw it coming, why didn't I see this coming?' moaned the unfortunate, deserted man.

I stepped it up a notch.

'Well darling, that's because you are a man,' said his new self-appointed counsellor. I now had his full attention. And that of several others I suspected. I swear I don't set out to do this. It just happens. His eyes now beseeched me for wisdom. I knew I was wasting my time but thought what the hell, I'm bored.

'Well, this is how it goes, a woman gets up in the morning and thinks about the relationship, she has breakfast and thinks about the relationship, she takes the kids to school and thinks about the relationship, she has coffee with friends and thinks about the relationship, she goes to work and thinks about the relationship and then she comes home, gets tea, washes the dishes watches a little television and she is still thinking about the relationship'

I paused here and was a little chagrined to find all eyes on me and the woman who had been copiously going through the Kleenex had stopped crying and was staring, open-mouthed at me also.

'But you,' I continued, 'get up and have breakfast and think about breakfast, you go to work and think about work, you have a few beers with your mates and think about your mates, you come home and read the newspaper and think about the newspaper, you watch TV and think about the TV program—your wife has had twenty years up on you of thinking about this and working it out and it's over sweetheart!'

And about his time the timid chuckles of the Kleenex lady had joined with the snorts from her friend and as the newly informed man went back to his confused reverie we women had a wonderful chat and the tissues were handed around to all for the laughter instead.

Social Distancing Please!

At the supermarket. I'd been to Barossa Food Wonderland a few times in the time of Covid and found that all the customers and servers were social distancing as if they were in the Russian Ballet. All natural grace, and polite nodding.

Until one Tuesday in summer. A checkout woman past the classification of 'chick' was serving customers with all the gusto of a philharmonic conductor and repeating, 'Social Distancing, please,' as if she just discovered the words and was so enamoured with their poetic beauty that she had to repeat the phrase frequently, along with an extravagant gesture that would have made goat herders weep with envy.

I approached and began to stack my items on the conveyor noting that her current customer was at least two metres away at the end of the line packing items into her trolley. The checkout woman was a slow as a wet week. She wasn't watching the items as they passed over the blipper as she was heavily engaged in conversation with the customer who was about ten inches from her as they shared their pain at not being able to make use of their brand new caravans purchased pre-Covid, 'if only we'd known.'

They sounded as if they were lifelong friends but may have only just met – supermarkets are like that. One had aborted a trip to Darwin, the other had a yen for The Peninsula.

The items passed the scanner, the scanner blipped, goodness knows how many of the items were missed or scanned twice.

Checkout woman noticed me, 'Social Distancing, please,' she said, waving her arm with the snide smirk of a rental evictor. I rolled the milk bottles onto the conveyor. She rolled her eyes.

A woman in the queue behind me moved forward. Checkout woman waved an imperious arm and repeated 'Social Distancing, please,' until the poor woman was halfway down the pet food aisle.

The two at the end continued their dissertation on travel-hunger in a time of Covid. The customer had blue ticking bags with strange white strings attached. Checkout woman struggled with these contraptions and broke one of the dangling strings before loading another bag. She then asked, 'Would you like the rest of your items bagged?'

I stared at the two pineapples on the conveyor belt and made a rough guess that the woman didn't want to carry them out of the shop under her arm. The woman nodded. Bags, yes.

By this time the customer halfway down the pet food aisle had galloped off to another line and was heading for the carpark.

A gentleman in a wheelchair approached the line. 'Social Distancing, please,' she informed him. He looked at the woman then at the controls. I don't think he'd thoroughly conquered reverse. He stared at a can he was holding then at the conveyor belt.

'Any good at basketball?' I enquired politely.

He grinned and stopped his efforts to reverse his wheelchair.

'Social Distancing, please,' said Madam Checkout, clearly aiming for a position in management or government.

When I finally arrived at the checkout, the daft woman leaned forward to get my card. It took all my self-control to refrain from—'Social Distancing, please.'

Doctor's office reception room

The room was too small. The lights too bright, a thousand watts or more, lasering tired eyes and flimsy nerves. The outdoors too near, more inside than out. You could see half the town, people walking, dogs with heads on paws resigned to long waits on leashes, eyebrows flinching.

The place would've been better as a goldfish bowl, for guppies seeking to linger, kissing glass edge, eyeing humans and pondering what made them stare at fish in bowls. The chairs were too close together, rooms too close to each other. The people were strange with no sense of order, or queuing. No respect for silence or smells or loud scrapings. Sniffing and coughing, gouging out what was left of the quietitude.

The toys were placed on noise enhancing floor, or there was an infant with extraordinary strength banging and thumping toys that rattled with metallic exuberance and clattered and deafened and shredded nerves further.

The floor was too noisy with its linoleum cheapness, its fierce economy and insulting thinness, a poor skin for cement, hard and cold. There were too many doors hiding hallways and corridors, with heels smacking down them, while echoes chased echoes.

The receptionist's desk was too high and remote with the tired, sick and miserable far below, seeking comfort and quiet and forced to yell symptoms and diseases to brisk secretaries who would then find patient records that guaranteed privacy. But what's the use of that when she asked why are you here? why do you want the doctor? Did she expect a few to say, it's just a social call, I was just passing and thought I'd drop by? But no, poor old gents lent forward with hoarse whispers and muttered, I'm having troubling whizzing. But she can't hear and asks again. So phlegm scratching cough and he repeats a bit louder, I can't take a piss, then subsides into silence and shrugs at his wife, who's scanning the room for magazines and wondering if she's read that New Idea, or not.

There are stupid conversations on the right and the left. The sneezing old man with rampant nose hair sits too close, wet germ soaked handkerchief tucked in a pocket, not retreating, and the kid with the toy with coloured balls on curved wires bashes it again and again on the floor, then when his mother stops this satisfying activity, he screams louder than toys until she gives it back and it begins again, the screech and thundering.

There was a sign on the wall that offered false promise—wait no longer than 20 minutes. The chairs are lined up the wrong way, like seats on a bus. A doctor comes out of the room opposite. No, please not him, he looks like an unkempt gardener who couldn't tend a row of beans. How will he know about the subtleties of mental trauma? He doesn't seem careful so how could he care about people and maladies that belong in the head but fall out, run around, create havoc and can't be tamed or corralled or ridden – get back in the saddle. He calls out. My son rises.

Oh bother, it's for him, for us. Inside the doctor asks questions so puerile and inane that I wonder if this is all a practical joke and perhaps he is the gardener. The platitudes come quickly. Were you bullied at school, he asks, not solemnly but with curiosity common in bored housewives or persons with little to do. Yes, says my son, he's no good at lies, although I think he'd rather be somewhere else. What happened for that to stop, he asks and if I was watching a television show I'd laugh out loud.

My son is as big as a mountain, a chest like Mike Tyson, but he doesn't state the obviously, merely politely says quietly, I grew, up.

He asks, 'What worried you today. Coming here, doing this, police. Ah he pounces, staring down his narrow nose, why the police, eyeing the mountain as if he might have been tempted to gang bash someone or do a ram raid if he had time, but my son meekly says, you get fined $500 for not wearing a seatbelt in this state and the doctor sighs, seeming disappointed. He has a dull job.

This intrusive dill continues pushing his questions as if my son is docile and dim and poorly presenting, not knowing the huge patience and kind-heartedness and definitely not the intelligence. I know my son is struggling to work out if the problem is with him, or the doctor.

When we leave he drives, he's very quiet, cogitating.

I can't take any more and say, he's an idiot, I rant and get up full steam. Never going there again and the condescension, patronising git of man.

My son sighs a full sigh, full chested and relieving and mutters, he couldn't even decide if he was going to go bald or not.

I break out laughing, such a funny thing to mention. I explain that the doctor had had plastic surgery, hair transplant. I explain the procedure and my son is amazed.

Aha,' That explains the rows, the symmetry, he says.

It's only been half an hour but it seems like six months. I've walked in his shoes, maybe one mile or two. I've been hyper-stimulated, noise confronted, confused, insulted, misunderstood and bemused. I've been autistic for a morning and I don't much like it.

I don't know how he does it. Day after day.

Ingredients for disaster

Cars. Petrol. Electricity. Speed. Proximity to other vehicles. Crazy persons behind the wheel. Quirks of nature like hole in the road, landslides and sink holes. To name a few. It's a wonder there aren't more accidents. I mean, there you are barrelling down a highway, going faster than a cheetah with only a metre or between you and the next vehicle. I won't lie. I've had a few accidents. After all, I lived in Sydney – that paradise for disaster, and, I was a community nurse so lots of motoring.

Accident Number One. I'm driving in the rain, waiting at a precarious spot after leaving Warner's Bay. Not trusting mirrors, I wind my window down and poke my head out into the rain. Bang. I'm hit from behind. My right eyebrow bumps the window frame. I turn the corner, pull to the side. The other driver is a young woman who has just purchased her first car after only having her license for a few weeks. She's distraught, flapping her hands in front of her. I get out of the car to console her.

Unfortunately, the eyebrow bump chooses that moment to release enough blood to soak a doona. I don't notice it, but the poor girl shrinks down and cries. She was terrified of telling her father, the cops, well, just about everyone. I looked at my car. There's a bit of a dent. I really don't care. She's alright. I'm alright.

I'm not a "car person". I never worshipped a car. Was bored spitless when my friends watched the Bathurst 500. If it goes it goes. I've seen the abysmal angst in new car owners with that first, in my opinion INEVITABLE, dent. People weeping like paid mourners at a funeral over a bit of plastic that has barrelled towards disaster every day it's on the road. You'd think their firstborn had been kidnapped. I've always thought that when you first buy a car you should have a little hammer, make a little dent and get the whole nonsense out of the way. You're basically driving an incendiary device. Look at the road toll.)

I feel a trickle of blood down my face and understand the girl's reaction. 'Never mind that,' I say, 'let's look at your car. Not a scratch. That's good news.'

This doesn't have the effect of soothing her. 'The police,' she says, mentally going through the Road Rules in her head. 'We have to call them. And. Insurance! Oh God.'

'Why,' I say, 'why would we bother the boys in blue? Insurance, whatever for?'

I introduce her to a whole new philosophy of leaving things alone, which has obviously not been in her playbook before.

'But your car?' she whimpers.

'Oh never mind that – it matches the dent where I backed into my own house.'

Terracotta glory

The great-uncles

With the chill of the night at our backs we leaned towards the warmth of the fire. The pinecones we'd collected from the forest at Mr Pleasant glowed like amber Christmas trees. The blackened saucepan was on the boil. My favourite Italian sugar sat beside a small jug of milk on a wooden chopping board on the ground in a sheltered corner of the courtyard. Bronson put two English Breakfast teabags in my mug.

'What are you having?' I asked.

'Pine needle tea,' he said, 'it has more Vitamin C than anything else.'

'Good grief.' I smiled and pulled the pine needles off the branch beside me.

'Make sure you take the brown woody bits off Mum.'

I wrenched the pine needles into bunches and made a small pile on my knee. 'Ok, but if this pine needle tea tastes like the stuff on my hands I don't like the chances of it being a hit.'

An ordinary night, with the usual stars ... or perhaps not. The fire danced in an old beer keg Bronson had triumphantly brought home. He'd made a hole in the top and a perfect rectangle at the front. 'Ripper fire, Bronson.'

'Try the pine needle tea Mum.'

'That's not half bad.'

'Told you,' said Bronson. We watched the fire, silently sipping tea.

'Your father thought you and I were funny – he often found us sitting staring at the fire when he came home. You were hardly able to sit up. You leaned on me and we'd watch the flames with the wood heater door open.'

'Huh, we still love it.'

'Nothing like it really.'

'Mum, it's your birthday soon. You had the same birthday as Uncle Gordon didn't you. He died just after your birthday, and just before I was born. A few days. Wish I'd met him. You had great uncles, hey Mum.'

I cradled the warm mug and let the memories flow. I smiled at his phrase, they were his Great-uncles, but my great, wonderful uncles. Rare men.

It was time to tell him tales of the uncles. I began with his namesake. 'Even though you never met Uncle Gordon was there when I got the news I was pregnant. He often came and stayed with us in Coffs Harbour. Even when he was sick with prostate cancer he took your brother on a helicopter ride - and love it. Tough as old boots he was.' Bronson laughed, 'He loved lamb sandwiches, didn't he. We saw plenty of sheep today- that's why you said 'that's a lot of lamb sandwiches on those hills'. You must have hated to see him sick.'

'Yes, I drove down from Coffs many times - for his heart attack and cancer. Sweetest man. He had to have a kidney scan once and the radiologist came and got me to sit with him because it was taking so long for the dye to go through. I knelt on the floor. He wanted to give me his pillow, but I said I already had one. It was the only lie I ever told him. I held his big brown hand and we talked. About how special his life was, how grateful he was - for the little things. He didn't have much. Never wanted much. He sent all his pay home for his mother when he was at war. I stayed there an hour and a half before the scan was finished. I knew then his kidneys were shot. I was worried about him, but I think he was just as worried about my silly knees. I was glad my friend Andie was with me because I had Uncle Cliff that day too.'

'Crikey, how did you have two of them at the X-ray?'

'Uncle Cliff was staying with Mum. She was busy so I was minding him, he had a bit of dementia, (probably more than a bit) but we had to take him with us. He talked to everyone in the waiting room. Andie was Uncle Gordon's Veteran nurse, but because Uncle Gordon needed me, she was left with Uncle Cliff discussing his finances with a roomful of sick strangers.'

'Jeez. What was Uncle Cliff like? - before, I mean.'

'So very kind. He was quite different from Uncle Gordon in lots of ways, keen business man, played the organ.' I laughed.

'What's funny about that?'

'Well, nothing really. It's just that the Aunts were forever getting bees in their bonnets with each other, falling in and out, having bones to pick - or getting out of the wrong side of the bed... But the men, they were always the same. Uncle Cliff came up from Sydney every fortnight when Mum was looking after my Nana in our spare room after she'd had a stroke. Every time he came he gave Mum the rent money they missing because they couldn't rent out that part of the house, and a bit extra. When Nana died, he gave Mum all that was left because she had cared for their mother. Mum never forgot that.'

'Wow, that's something.' Bronson stoked the fire. 'What about the Brooks' uncles? Tell me about your Uncle Cec. How come I don't remember meeting him?' asked Bronson.

'You were only eight months old. It was when you were in Toowoomba Hospital with Stephen Johnson Syndrome.'

'Oh.' Bronson breathed the word as a sigh. He'd heard the story, but he hadn't realised the serious nature of the illness until he'd mentioned it to the blokes at work. 'Holy Crap,' they'd said, 'nobody gets over that, you're one lucky bastard, Sunshine' and this frank statement, along with a few of their own stories had more impact that a mother's tale of fear and angst. He came home in a thoughtful mood the day of that conversation. 'Oh, that.'

A routine early morning nappy change began one of the most terrifying days of my life. A large chunk of skin came off in my hand as I flipped the nappy aside. It was a hot summer day but my heart froze. By the time we rushed to our GP, Bronson was screaming. When the doctor examined his eyes, layers of skin peeled off Bronson's eyelids. The horror continued. Where ever he was touched deep layers of skin fell away.

He was rushed to hospital. Specialists from London and afar were consulted. Bronson had Stephen Johnson's Syndrome – 'cotton-wool baby'. He looked like a zombie. Worse was to follow, his mouth was ulcerated, along with his entire gut. Had it spread to his lungs? X-rays were needed, but Bronson clung to me like a terrified Koala. They couldn't take him so he was x-rayed in my arms. His lungs were untouched. The only other areas unscathed were the soles of his feet. He was in agony. They gave him a quarter of the adult male dose of Pethidine. It didn't touch him.

The doctors told us that most babies didn't recover. This may be a lifetime condition. However, they threw everything they had at him. They consulted with other hospitals, other international specialists – most babies had to live cocooned cotton wool. They gave him cortisone, adrenaline, painkillers and creams, but every touch was a nightmare. His father and I were gutted – our baby might not live. His brother torn with anxiety. I roomed in at the hospital. My mother came to stay. After an agonising week the screaming stopped and small signs of recovery began.

'We hadn't been in Toowoomba for long. We hadn't met many people, but we had a beautiful family that just took us into their home and hearts – Michael and Vanessa.' I explained to Bronson.

'Oh yeah, I'll never forget THEM, they gave me a game and were great – I played with Adi and Becky.'

'They were just wonderful. They brought clothes in and just did all sorts of quiet things no one else noticed. They were family, really.'

'I thought this was a story about my Great-uncle Cec?'

'Uncle Cec lived hours away, but when he heard you were sick he came straight away and sat from dawn to dark with me. Held me in his arms while I cried my heart out. He was so calm and beautiful. He had a voice like mellow whiskey, warm soft and raspy. A real man.'

'Don't think you know what you're talking about with the whiskey, Mum, but he sounds like a lovely man.'

'The best. Absolutely the best.'

Daniel

After two beers he was social, after four he was Donald Trump. Then after six, he was Socrates, slurring the phrase—'I have profoundness in me.' He'd done time. Nine years of it. The words 'misunderstood', 'assault' and 'substance use' crept into the meandering conversation.

He was my boarder. I only found out the former facts by accident. I usually went to my own section of my home as soon as I heard the clinking of the first stubby opening. Friendly and courteous - still there was something that set off my radar. So I retreated.

On the night of his revelations a friend had come to visit and we all sat on the back patio. With a companionable audience the facts slipped into the exchange. It was on that night I realised the source of my misgivings. His past. The soothing effects of the alcohol, along with my friends' non-judgemental responses dulled his ability to see the fear building within me. He informed my friend that he 'wasn't really smoking - the cigarettes were herbal, legal, bought at the local tobacconist. 'They're bath salts,' he said.

My friend, who worked in a drug and alcohol clinic read the 'ingredients', and said later that they were 'just bath salts'.

'Rubbish,' I said. 'No-one smokes bath salts.'

I later read a Marie Claire article and my suspicions were confirmed. Illegal drugs were not only ahead of the law, they were ahead of science. One molecule changed to push the product over the line into 'legal'.

I didn't know what to do, so I did nothing.

From the cocoon of my solace I heard long and enthusiastic phone calls as he paced the back patio for most of the night. His words only dimly penetrated my peace, so I left him be. Sometimes I heard parts of the conversations. There were grand words, interjected with 'you know I can do this, mate' 'I'm good for this'.

Forbidden to see his children, he was suffering. They were the lights of his life, but the pull of a world of drugs was too strong. He didn't understand, he thought he was clean - he believed his own illusions. He was 'okay'.

He was adopted and adored his adoptive parents, sad for the grief he had caused them over the years, remorseful for his bad decisions.

I often conversed briefly with him. He was quite shy before he'd torn the plastic coating from the huge slab of beer – the amber draught that gave him confidence and numbed the vulnerability – if he imbibed enough. He worried that he would never do anything good when the effects of his 'medications' were not blunting his thoughts. Most of all he yearned to see his children. At those times he accepted that he probably didn't deserve them, but wished they could know him. The best of him that had been forgotten – the best that he was yet to find.

'I can't find words,' he sighed. 'I wish I could write, like you do. Then I could give my girls something, just something good.' His hands trembled. He held a tattered notebook. There was a longing in his eyes as he stood before me, fumbling with the worn pages. And then I knew. He'd been writing, and was afraid. I didn't know what to say, so I said nothing.

Then with courage growing he held the book up for me to see clearly. 'I can't believe I'm doing this when I'm stone cold sober,' he said, voice ragged. 'Would you please read this for me?'

'Of course,' I said, sensing the importance of the moment.

'But you have to promise me something...'

'Yes?'

'You'll tell me the honest God's truth. Promise me that.'

'I promise. How long have you...'

'I started writing in jail, you know. I wrote for my girls. It's just a story...' Abruptly he turned away. I heard the hiss of a stubby opening.

Intrigued, but somewhat apprehensive, I took the notebook to my rooms and locked the door as I always did. I opened the book. The words resembled a school notebook, but unlike my negligent scribble, Dan had tediously formed the words. In careful print, no cursive 'running writing'. The words were uneven and hard to read. But I sat in my solitary lounge chair and entered the world of Dan.

After the first few dozen lines I was captivated. An English teacher would have covered the page with red pen corrections for grammar and spelling, but this wasn't school. This was life. Dan's. It was the story of two pigeons who fell in love. Two pigeons from different parts of the world. One was a racing pigeon and the other an ordinary pigeon who lived under the Sydney Harbour Bridge.

It was beautiful. He wept when I told him, reading the honesty in my eyes.

I typed the story and gave it to him to see if he liked the corrections, explaining that I'd only fixed his spelling and grammar.

'This is a real gem,' I said, 'I don't always read the books I put together for other people, but I love this story. Writing isn't about putting words together, but speaking from who you are. It would be such a gift for your girls.'

'That's all I want,' he said.

We chose photos, in that brief period after he'd returned from a long days' work, and before the slab called. Sometimes he would become allow bigger dreams to filter in – a movie, like no other. Animated by Pixar, produced by Disney. A blockbuster. At other times the tears would shine in his eyes as he spoke of having something worthwhile to give his girls.

I learned he had a significant knowledge about pigeons. The narrative had substance – his research and experience were compelling. But there was something else - as I read more of the awkward writing, I found grace. Two loving pigeons fighting life's battles side by side, and raising a son. A son who dreamed of becoming a racing pigeon. A little baby bird that was rescued by a mangy cat and a pelican on his first disastrous flight from the nest.

I worked on the story, wanting to bring it to print. Dan held back. It had to be more than right. It had to be perfect. He couldn't embrace my belief that the words had a power beyond 'perfect', and a purpose in the gift they would one day be to his girls.

Dan's late night phone calls and pacing increased. His 'bath salt' intake rose. The rubbish bin groaned under the weight of the empty beer bottles. The loud conversations began to last until 5 am, just hours before he was due at work.

One day he came home at lunchtime. He'd been assessed and fired. His behaviour became increasingly erratic. I was worried and fearful. I didn't know what to do, so I did nothing. The tone of his phone calls changed, they became more desperate; pleading. I never knew who was at the end of the line on those many calls. None of his friends or workmates ever came to visit.

One evening when he was particularly wild-eyed and confused, he told me he was going home to his parents. He was 43, alone and in need again. The only constant in his life of turmoil was the unquestioning support of his parents.

Like a whirlwind he was gone. The room was left immaculate. There was no sign he ever been there apart from the empty bottles carefully place in the recycling bin. I was relieved when he left, but saddened. Who was he, really? His addictions and struggles? Or his desires and hopes? A man lost on the road to forgiveness? Perhaps all of them.

I tucked the folder with his story and files that were ready for printing into a small corner of my computer, wishing there was a way to tell Dan's story, but it was his. However, beautiful or worthy I felt the words were I had no right to publish his story.

I still love the narrative as much as when I first saw it. I don't know where Dan is, or how his life has been. I don't know what to do with his wonderful story, so I'm doing nothing, hoping that's what Dan would want. I relegated the story to the back of my mind, where it stays, apart from those deep and thoughtful moments when I wonder what the sum of a man is. Then, I linger awhile with the draft of the manuscript, and see the best of Dan.

Roof sealer

'I've got bad news,' he says. 'You'd better sit down.'

Now call me daft, but I took offence at this. I expect to hear this phrase from a policeman with cap in hand, looking solemn, yet compassionate on my doorstep. I expect to hear this from medical personnel wiping perspiration from their foreheads and looking like they might cry. I don't expect this nonsense from a man in a suit who climbed onto my roof, took some photos of my ageing cement tiles, colour—Nondescript Green on his iPad and counted to 25. A man who has walked through the door to my house is now telling me to take a seat. Really? How about I tell you if you can take a seat before you start catastrophizing about my roof or anything else.

The polite conversation in the front yard that had meandered towards the salesman's ultimate destination of telling me what I needed went downhill after sentence of doom so fast the poor guy was confused.

My mother dispatched salespersons faster than anyone I've ever known. 'What's in the suitcase?' she'd ask, bristling, as they began the charming spiel that left other store managers enchanted. 'Don't give me the runaround, just show me what you have to sell. I'm a busy woman.' And then if the sales rep kept rambling Mum simply went 'Pffft' and walked off.

Which is what I wanted to do, but the man was inside my house with his size 12 feet under my table, his iPad out and warming to the topic of my roof. Don't get me wrong. I'm interested in my roof. There's some mortar missing and I'd like a tradesman to do a bit of repair work. Full stop. And here's Mr Grey Suit with his pristine foldout ladder taken from his immaculate BMW prosing on. A man who has roamed my roof for precisely one minute in his Florsheim shoes. A man who hasn't seen the 52 page report by the building inspector that has beautiful colour photographs of every detail of my roof. And if that wasn't bad enough he begins a science lesson like nothing I've ever heard beginning with—'Your roof is painted'.

'Yes,' I say, 'no flies on you is there. It's an intriguing colour I like to refer to as Mildew.'

He baulks before moving into science. 'Paint is really only tint and water.'

'Oh dear, Mr Taubmans will be disappointed,' I say.

He hesitates before moving on to explain that 'cement is only sand and water – paint and mortar wash away.' He's in earnest now, closing in.

'I'd better go outside and check if the paths are still there,' I say, 'it's been raining rather heavily.'

He shows me photographs of chipped tiles. My chipped tiles.

'Well, those magpies will swoop anything,' I said, earning me a look normally given to the deranged.

He flicks on his iPad to photos of lichen and moss on my roof, expecting me to be apoplexic by now, or at least working up to a Cerebro-Vascular Accident.

'Isn't that adorable,' I say, 'not quite your English cottage look, but getting there.'

Undeterred, he moves on to explain that his company does something very different to solve all these issues. They apply a membrane. Now I'm a nurse and there's nothing more delicate than a membrane. Whoever came up with a sales pitch for a product requiring strength and endurance and calling it a membrane has lost the plot.

I've had enough. 'Write all that down, put it in an email and send it to me,' I say, and then because he doesn't seem to be catching on, I stand up and push the chair in. This he understands. Shuffling his papers he leaps to his feet, gapes like a guppy and leaves.

I have visions of men in suits glad-wrapping my house before driving off in BMWs and Bentley's while I wave them (and my money) a cheery goodbye.

The Tradesmen Wars

The painter

He came, he saw, he did not conquer.

I wanted the lattice work at my back patio painted white instead of the military green that I considered to be an eyesore. Sick of doing everything myself I organised to get a quote from a well-reviewed painter.

'No painter on earth would paint lattice,' he said, then fearing that my silence meant that I was profoundly deaf, added, 'Nobody in their right mind would think of painting lattice work.'

Naturally, I set about to paint lattice, aiming for 'improvement' rather than perfection.

The gate techo

The painter recommended his mate Jason to put a gate in. He came, he saw, and he conquered, making off with $600 in a quick retreat, which later seemed like an huge sum considering I supplied the materials. And...

There's the old saying 'If it waddles like a duck.... Quacks like a duck... it's a duck' isn't true for this apparatus; it looks like a gate ... however, it doesn't allow for that marvellous purpose of a gate, to allow a vehicle to have entrance into the property. It's too narrow, even for a modest Corolla. Perhaps it would suit a person requiring generous access for a wheelbarrow, or a bicycle.

The gate sections are growing tired, pulled by their weight into the middle, unconstrained by the correct proportions of cement footing, even though the cement mixed was made in my two buckets.

I don't have a gate. I don't have buckets. But somewhere out there, there's a guy with my dosh.

My son, astonished by my bad luck, said, 'Where do you find these people?'

I gave him a stern look, a pithy admonishment about victim blaming and told him I didn't know and was prone to blame the government for changing the name of the Fair Trading Department and pulling its teeth in the meantime.

Son, sensing an imminent Cause, asked what I meant to do about it, so I replied that after imagining all the dodgy tradespersons of my acquaintance making medical appointments only to find the doctor or nurse had gone to the Local pub I would make broad enquiries across State and Federal Legislature to find out why Govt decided to pull the teeth of Fair Trading and relegate their scope of work to 'mediation' which in 99% of cases had already failed.

Garage Re-Conversion

On careful scrutiny I found that all the power points were 'out', but not the lights or the town. Therefore, by deduction taught by my father - it had to be a fuse. In the fuse box that was safely walled in behind the roller door that was operated electrically, plugged in to a power point with no backup manual override. Botheration.

I considered the wisdom of taking a nap and while lying with closed eyes I realised I wouldn't be able to muster any help as twilight was coming sooner rather than later. I don't usually think I'll need any help for any given situation in life, unlike my mother who yahooed 'MAX!' every time some little thing went awry like the toaster not working because it wasn't plugged in. I understand theoretically that husbands have the capacity to be of use in varying degrees but experientially, not so much. Both husbands gave the impression that any disaster came under the heading of My Stuff that would interfere with the overload of His/Their Stuff that he/they were already stressed to the eyeballs. This was never a short, calm speech, but more along the lines of a tantrum that meandered to include every vicissitude of life in general and their job/recreational plans/obligations to persons other than a wife, along with a none too subtle theory that these events were created by said wife to ruin their lives. Humour was not appropriate at such times so staring at the floor got the lecture over with and resulted in a hasty exit from the premises and a lengthy period of time before their return to said abode. Husband No. 1 gave shorter 'lectures' and took the car. Husband No. 2 gave parliamentary addresses and went for excessively long walks. So seeking assistance isn't my first instinct in spite of the fact that I've enjoyed two sons with the blue collar skills and good humour of their patient grandfather.

This time however, I phoned Son No. 2 who had the usual rambling discussion that characterises our modus operandi for problem solving. I rang the builder who had sectioned off the garage. There was talk of manholes, tiles and creating openings into the shed space through the ceiling. Sadly solar panels vetoed the tile option as Son No. 2 surveyed the roof, giving me a heart attack by using a plastic bucket on top of a step ladder to secure entrance through the manhole. But why should I worry about a son who leaped off my house with his skateboard and when landing safely said, 'How about that! I'm still alive.' Clearly made of rubber and capable of holding his own in the Cirque de Soleil. I told him to go home and I'd phone the builder again. No answer. As soon as Son No. 2 left I jettisoned the bucket and stepladder arrangement, brought in the rusty ladder left by the previous owners and planned my next move. The axe had been broken in an attempt to lever the roller door high enough to fit a person under it so I got my tomahawk, purchased for me by Son No. 1 who vetoed most of my more ambitious ventures, took my phone in case the builder phoned while I was in the roofspace and got my torch.

Getting through the manhole was a doddle. And just like my life where I peaked in high school and everything was downhill from there, my agility and speed across the ceiling was arduous indeed. I knew just how large a hole could be left by a careless foot because Dad and I had used a bucket of spackle, yards of chicken wire and several newspapers to fill a hole made by Husband No. 1. So I crawled, along the beams, with an ouch ouch here and an ouch ouch there. I heard odd squeaking noises that could have been feathered or rodent. There were enough spider webs for an episode of the Adams Family. But I was a woman on a mission. Fruitless and unnecessary but a mission nonetheless. I made fastidious calculations once I arrived at the front of the house, got out the tomahawk and made quick work of creating a man-sized hole. But there was too much light, and bother, there was my car. I'd made a hole in the eaves at the front of the house. I didn't give up.

I was in the middle of recalculating when the builder phoned, always ready for my adventures. Nope to getting in through tile removal, nope to cutting a hole in ceiling gyprock – beams too close together for an adult. Might fit a small child, but child labour was illegal in spite of the benefit of size. Heard the beep on the phone that signified another caller. Bound to be Son No. 2 who had been impressed with my ascent. Builder suggested hole in new wall of garage conversion, ie, one layer gyprock, the layers hardiplank. Bother. Builder hangs up, he's miles away and can't join in. Cautions me against circular saw due to my novitiate skill in that regard. Son No. 2 phones. 'How'd you get up there?' Ladder, the rusty one. 'What possessed you to go and do something that had already been done by a 29 year old in peak fitness when you're 65?' The answer to that was False Pride but I didn't say that because it was also due to Irish genes that had those canny Celts signing up to fight alongside the British with not a skerrick of patriotism but for the money. NOT that anyone was going to pay ME, but I might save having to pay someone else, what with my current plan of being in the black, please God, for just one pension fortnight.

Hole in the wall it was, No 2 Son on the way with the cavalry, his inestimable and doubly patient wife. Son admired the pile of fibro and the shattered eave with consternation and mirth. Jeez Mum. I know. With meticulous placement of the right tools a hole was soon made by him, and his hand thrust through the hole, where the flaming fuse switch was back ON. I don't want to think of the fixing of the solution of the problem. I still can't get into the shed because the roller door now responds to the remote with squeaking and wiggling that would do justice to Miley Cyrus. In short it won't rise. So how the electricity man is going to read the meter is anathema. I haven't slept. Mr Clooney, the cat, excited from all the activity has come out from hiding under the bed and is galloping around the house like Phar Lap.

As I lay me down to sleep
I pray the Lord my soul to keep
and if my sacro-ileac makes me yell
I'll curse not, fear'd of a greater hell

and for those dear souls in states of confusion
wondering if my stories are imagined illusion
that I've misunderstood the meaning of progress
as they struggle to grasp the concept of regress

those wan souls acquainted with forward direction
where chaos and mayhem end up as perfection
because they haven't had the beleaguered occasion
where bedlam sublime arrives in spite of intention

and women, with those marvellous commodities
called husbands, should forget spousal oddities
recall a list of their better-half's contributions
say a prayer of thanks, or contrite absolution

and profess profound gratitude for forward motion
and for NOT BEING LINDA, knee-deep in commotion.

*NOTE One year after a garage conversion $$ I discovered that the work had not been council approved. ☹ Furthermore there was a hefty fine for owner and 'builder', so I'm dismantling... and may never mantle again.

I'd like to go outside and take photographs of weeds and debris in protest of the Facebook mythology that our lives are fulfilled, fabulous and near perfect. My wood heater is smoking more than Keith Richards in spite of the attentions of the equivalent of a chimney sweep, which may or may not be a trade. My kitchen tap has been leaking for over a year after installation by a plumber who is possibly shearing sheep or saving the economy by driving a truck. In any case he's incommunicado in spite of texts, phone messages and extremely pungent smoke signals. As for the Master and Commander of the walled in electricity meter, at a rough guess he's at Lego School or in protective custody. At his last visit he favoured talk over toolbelt and brought the negotiating passion of a salesperson extolling a used car without an engine as 'mint condition'. The expert aircon guy who came to relocate the outdoor unit pronounced that the gas compressor had died in spite of the fact that it was heating and cooling with quiet precision. I smiled, nodded and saw the grin of satisfaction cross his face that here was a ditzy woman who was eating up his BS (better to be underestimated than overestimated). He then went on to explain that he was now a sales rep of a rival company and could supply me with an efficient replacement for a few paltry thousands of $$. The roof seal repair guy prosed on about membranes and their superiority over more substantial repair products while standing in a pristine suit and Florsheim shoes.

It's a shock to a country girl who grew up with half a dozen family members who could, and did, fix anything, not least of all my father who carried the strong genetic blue-collar skills of half a dozen tradespersons as did his brothers, Ken and Cec Brooks. Even Mum's side of the family had good old 'Gorgie', (Gordon Stockdale) who may have driven below every speed limit in Christendom but could make lawnmowers and other motors sing.

It was enough of a shock to have a husband who, when he'd spend six weeks 'fixing' the clothes dryer was shocked to discover that the 'COOL' setting was now 'HOT' and vice versa. He was so enraged by the inadequacy of the dryer that he went for a ten mile calming walk. As he arrived back from said calming sojourn with as much ill temper as he left it was generally felt that even if he'd walked to Darwin it wouldn't have helped. So the rest of us took the opportunity to claim dire need of groceries and escape to the local mall for chips and a milkshake. The worst part of it was that there was nothing wrong with the dryer before his tempestuous ministrations. He took it off the wall, dismantled it into a thousand bits and spread it over the lounge room floor until a friend who visited often talked her husband into bringing a trailer and relocating the whole pile to the local tip.

When assisting a mechanic to dismantle the car engine, instead of placing the pistons in order on a numbered piece of cardboard designated by the qualified mechanic, he placed them randomly on the wrong piece of cardboard, stunning his friend into silence—until he went to the default position of abusing the objects instead of offering contrition. The noise of this rant caused the mechanic to quietly, yet swiftly, leave the premises. His departure was unnoticed by the cranky assistant for some time. This time a calming walk was the only option as the car was literally in bits. At least when he emptied the contents of a gas bottle into the air in the suburbs the car was available for me to escape under the guise of having run out of milk.

After a lifetime of singing the praises of tradesmen I'm over the gormless muddling of the inept, unreliable minority. I'm over the pretty posts, the living the best life blarney and as soon as the sun comes up I'm going outside to take photos of weeds, broken bricks, random rubble, rubbish that is too 'hard' for the council hard rubbish cleanup, and you'll just have to live with it.
*anyone reading should remember that the truth negates the litigious option of defamation.

Three billy goats gruff

'I can't walk.' Jemima's furious approach up Ellie's driveway stalled

'Well, how'd you get here then?' asked Ellie.

Jemima's face flushed red.

Ellie sighed. Her response had obviously fallen short – in fact it went no distance at all towards appeasing the angry woman in front of her. Jemima was here for a fight and none was forthcoming. Her declaration about being unable to walk was intended to make Ellie feel guilty that someone who'd had endured three 'useless goes' at back surgery had been forced to walk two whole streets to 'speak her mind'. Ellie had heard all this before, the agony of a young woman not yet forty needing a four pronged walking stick – which she had forgotten in her haste to arrive at Ellie's house.

'If you had something to say to me, Jemima, you could have just phoned.'

'The phone's been... I... it's not working.'

Ellie shrugged. Jemima's constant struggle to pay the bills and care for her four children had been part of an afternoon that was intended as the two women getting to know each other, but had mainly comprised the cataloguing of Jemima's woes. Ellie had listened attentively to the recitation of the history of Jemima's pain levels and the long list of medications necessary to help her get through the day. She'd murmured sympathetically until Jemima began to explain the last operation in great detail including the insertion of twelve inch steel rods along her spine. Ellie felt more than a little squeamish. She could take no more. 'Didn't they give you an anaesthetic? I can't imagine remembering something that traumatic in such detail,' she said, and was rewarded with a sour look. However, the remark had the desired effect and Jemima diverted from the procedural description, but sadly not the subject.

'Why do you use big words? Are you trying to make me feel small? You don't know what it's been like,' said Jemima. 'I've had three years of hell.'

'Life can be tough. My mother lives with us – she's had a stroke,' said Ellie, hoping this sharing would comfort Jemima. Apparently not. Jemima pursed her lips.

'Were you in a car accident?' asked Ellie, attempting to make amends.

Jemima blushed. 'No, I picked the laundry basket up the wrong way.'

'Oh... yes, well, that must have been the last straw...'

Jemima frowned, then went on to enlarge on the topic and Ellie wondered how a simple visit to get to know the mother of a school friend of her 12 year old son could turn into a one sided monologue that had her struggling to keep her breakfast down.

It might be a bit old fashioned, but Ellie followed the simple philosophy of you can't visit anyone's house until I've met the parents. That first phone call to establish contact with Skye's mother hadn't been straightforward. 'I'm Ben's mother. He and your daughter Skye are in the same class and they've become friends. She's been over at my place and...

'Oh, I wondered where she was,' said Jemima, 'that's nice.'

'Well, I just thought it would be nice for us to meet.'

'Who? You and me?'

'Yes, just to...'

'Why? Do you want to check up on me?'

Ellie hesitated. She wasn't going to be politically correct and say 'no, of course not', she'd had enough of that in life. 'I like to know where my son is, and who he's with – I'm sure you'll be happier to know the same about Skye.'

Jemima muttered a time to call and vague words that even the most optimistic soul would have difficulty seeing in a welcoming light. But Ellie had accepted and shown up with her best smile and nonjudgmental face, then spent two hours in Jemima's dimly lit dining room.

Ben and Skye became inseparable. Apparently they couldn't breathe without each other. Sometimes one of Skye's two large teenage brothers came to tell her to 'get home now'. Ellie was relieved that the two seemed content to visit at her house. Ben's requests to go over to Skye's had died out – perhaps something to do with the two large brothers. The two were sitting desk to desk at school.

Ellie watched their two heads together and felt a little uneasy. Skye seemed to turn up every afternoon and on weekends. Ben's other friends were dropping away. She worried that they were too young to spend so much time together, but she remembered a physics class on 'everything having an equal and opposite reaction' - if she just gave it enough time.

The pendulum swung. Insults were traded. Recriminations hurled. Ben reported shouting matches at school. He began to get off the bus closer to home. When Ellie heard that Skye's brothers had joined the fray she decided to do something. A quick phone call to the class teacher sorted the situation. Desks were separated. The classroom divided in two. If either child was in the wrong half there would be trouble. The two children settled. Ellie sent a grateful prayer to the saint of teachers. The romance of the century was over, and the war of words had died. So, why in the name of all that was sane, was Jemima standing in front of Ellie, breathing fire.

'I can't believe you've forbidden your son to see my daughter!'

'Trust me. They don't want to lay eyes on each other for the rest of their natural lives.'

'They loved each other.'

'They're twelve.' Ellie was more amused than upset, which only made matters worse.

'You don't have the right,' spat Jemima.

'This isn't Romeo and Juliet. They...'

'There you go again. Talking down to me. I've had enough,' said Jemima, turning on her heel.

'Do you want me to drive you? Save you walking...'

Jemima picked up the pace, too angry to respond - or to limp.

Half an hour later there was a knock on the door. It was the fifteen year old younger brother – towering over Ellie. 'I want to see your son and have it out with him.'

'Oh, I don't think so, Sunshine,' said Ellie.

'I WILL see him,' said the lumbering boy, putting his hand on the screen door knob.

'In case you haven't noticed – this is MY house, and I get to say who does what. Comprendez?'

Speechless, the boy left.

Ellie went to water the garden. Along came the older brother, an even larger boy. 'This is getting to be like The Three Billy Goats Gruff,' Ellie said to him. The teenage mountain stopped. He stood confused.

'Did your brother tell you what I told him?' asked Ellie.

The startled boy nodded.

'Then I'll just say 'ditto', you can go home and everything will be sorted, okay?'

The boy left. Ellie finished watering the garden.

November lilies

Uncle Artie

My mother's Uncle Artie was a wealthy horse racing identity with his own stud farm. I only met him once and the memory is very hazy. We didn't visit often because Uncle Artie, for all his worldly endowments, was not held in high regard. I once asked my mother why.

'He gambles,' she said succinctly, expecting me to arrive at enlightenment.

I didn't, which brought out one of my own fatal flaws, that of not 'leaving well enough alone'. My next question of 'What's gambling?' prompted a lengthy treatise on the evils of 'throwing your money after a mangy nag and leaving your family to starve'. This only served to confuse me more, because that one visit to Uncle Artie's had left the impression that not even the cat had known one day of hunger.

'What does he gamble on?' was my next foray deeper into unknown terrain. Terrain that was 'fast wearing thin a person's patience'. However, my education was high on my mother's agenda so she persevered with me.

'He gambles on horse races,' said Mum with some finality.

'Whose horses?'

'*HIS* horses. He owns thoroughbred racing horses.'

'Oh. So Uncle Artie bets money on horses that he's trained hard to win? And he's rich.'

Mum didn't appear to like the direction of this conversation. 'That's one way to put it. But he's been very lucky,' said Mum, 'which is more than anyone can say for poor schmucks like us.'

I walked away still confused on the matter of Uncle Artie's 'gambling'. A few lessons on probability in Maths soon had me sorted on the question of 'odds'. In the end, Mum made sense. I had no luck picking names out of a hat at school.

Serious gambling just isn't for me. After all, every time I go to the supermarket and pick the shortest aisle, I find I've chosen the one that will take the longest time. I groan as I hear, 'Price check on Aisle 3.' Mind you, I still maintain a certain fondness for the idea of betting on yourself. Now that's 'a horse of a different colour.

It's not about the pudding

Every year was the same. In spite of my best intentions Christmas turned into a shambles. In our family, I'm a bit like 'whatsisname', the grubby boy from Charlie Brown who manages to get covered in grime every time he leaves his front door, much to the dismay of Lucy. Lucy is fastidiously clean, tidy, well-presented and permanently in a bad mood. Perhaps they all go together. The experience of being the only perfect person in the mix must make for some sour feelings. I was doomed to failure when compared with those sublimely addicted to the flawless performance of the Christmas rituals - or any rituals at any other time actually.

I'm sure many homes have Yuletide fiascos. A choice slice of martyrdom is served up alongside the Christmas bird. It is as inevitable as any other part of the tradition. Even if you make a pact with the lady of the house to have no presents - there will be presents. If you organise paper plates, there will be extra cutlery. If you bring plastic cups and cutlery, there will be three tablecloths and several dinner sets needed. That's the thing with Asperger's. Although addicted to rules and routines, they are often the first to change their expectations of others at the drop of a hat, then berate you for getting it wrong.

Christmas a few years ago was no exception. That year I decided on the ice-cream Christmas pudding. I hoped it would go some distance towards breaching the gap between the expectations of a perfect day, and the pathetic standard that I am actually able to meet. Things fell apart after the meal, but it wasn't about the pudding.

I managed to incur the wrath of my mother more than usual. Most years I did this by getting nervous when everything is going well, and giggling too much - or at the wrong things. And all without the effects of alcohol – no, we don't have *that* kind of Christmas 'spirit'.

I remember as a child that humour was rare, and mainly provided by the dry wit of my father. As children we got quite drunk on mirth in the way you do when something is funny, but there is the heightened sense that it could all be over in a second. Our ears would be soundly boxed, then off to the bath. We'd be in bed dizzy with the speed it took. On one occasion my brother suggested we sing 'Kiss me Goodnight, Sergeant Major', which we proceeded to do rather loudly. The danger was spine tingling. This was one of the moments that endeared me to my older brother when I was a child. The fact that I was *not* currently endeared to him was the sticking point. Whether the yuletide phone call from my brother was orchestrated to occur in the short time I was off-duty, and present at my mother's unit hardly matters. I was alone in the dining room. With her usual theatric approach, my mother came back to the dining room and announced loudly, 'If anyone else wants to talk to Evan they had better come now.'

When my mother wanted to make a point she referred to us as 'anyone', 'someone', or 'a person'. Mum favoured the less personal approach when making requests. It's an Asperger's thing. Her favourite phrases included, 'If someone would make me a sandwich, I would eat it.' if you are standing to leave the room, just as you get near her she will say, apparently to no-one in particular - 'If anyone is going to the kitchen they can take my plate.' This habit caused the rest of us much mirth. Mirth that was treated with disdain and sniffling aloofness. She didn't handle humour where she was the object of the amusement.

When Mum made her announcement to the room empty of all but me, I answered even though not 'personally addressed'. This was an old game we played. I never learned the good sense to ignore questions or statements addressed to 'anyone'. I ploughed right into the conflict with the first thought that came to hand - incidentally also the truth. 'I have said all I need to in that direction. Anyway, I doubt he wants to speak to me.'

This was not the answer she wanted. The sugar plum fairy had danced in her head and she had other ideas. Namely, me building bridges. Not the kind of bridge where the gap is actually spanned, but where we pretend and go back to the 'comfortable' dysfunction of the past. I was having none of that. Even though she dropped the subject for a nano-second I noticed the over-bright eyes, the rigidness of stance, and should have known it wasn't over. While she had me held prisoner lying on the couch, she delivered her Christmas Lament. 'It's Christmas!' She paused for that bit of news to sink into my obviously thick head. 'It's the time of peace and forgiveness; it is the time to forgive and forget.'

I wasn't greatly inclined to listen to her high and mighty advice as she had been central to creating the problem in the first place. 'Forgiving people who feel they've done nothing wrong only insults the hell out of them.' This didn't go very far towards appeasing my mother. Even though she had spent most of the last 30 or years lamenting that my brother *never* came to her at Christmas, I was not allowed to curry any ill-favour towards him myself.

The best Christmas occurred when everyone was there, thus leaving no-one to be the sacrificial lamb. It also helped that Mum made that most wonderful of blunders and bought alcoholic cider instead of the usual non-alcoholic and got a little merry indeed.

With Mum standing over me, I sensed a subtle shift from being the target of the Lament, to actually being the cause of it. All was lost for another year at least.

Mum's get-rich-slow schemes

'You could help me, Lin,' Mum said, waving a piece of paper. 'There's a fete at the community centre. They have all sorts of stalls. We could do with the extra money. You're good at all kinds of things.'

'But you never sell everything you make. That's hardly profitable.'

Mum handed me the paper. 'It would be lovely to do something together,' she said. 'You're always making something anyway. Why not pool our resources. We might make a bit of money, you never know.'

I rolled my eyes. 'Sounds like a *get rich slow scheme* to me.'

'Trust you to be sarcastic.'

'Oh Mum, it's a lot of work. Are retired people supposed to slow down?'

'Don't be silly. Slow down and you die.'

'See this,' she jabbed the page. 'We could have a stall. We could do arts and crafts.'

'Yeah, we all know that leads to untold wealth.'

Mum's eyes narrowed. 'You can't just bury your talents in the ground,' she said.

'I know what I could bury in the ground,' I said. Thankfully, due to my mother's poor hearing she didn't catch this remark.

'They only take five percent of your profits, that's fair.' Mum smiled triumphantly. 'You'll see.'

I pulled a face. Or maybe you'll see I thought, imagining Mum discovering the futility of hours spent over a sewing machine, knitting or crocheting. 'All right, let's do it,' I said. 'But I can't...'

'No such word as can't.'

'People to have limitations, Mum.'

'Rubbish, limitations are for lazy people. Let's start. Here's what I think...'

I over-locked facecloths so she could crochet around them. I made aprons, bibs and, back opening shirts for 'the elderly'. We had stalls at markets. She held stalls in the main street. But I put my foot down at that malarkey. Mum came up with an endless array of handcrafts. We shopped for materials.

'Jeez, Mum. This stuff costs more than we'd make on it.'

Mum gave me The Look. This was reserved for me alone. I called it the 'You're A Right Smart Arse' look.

Early in life Mum and I had parried over a million subjects. Dad's assessment was that neither of us knew when to leave well enough alone. He was, of course, right. I began as a toddler with questions: of 'Why can't my cat talk?' 'Does God wear pyjamas?' 'Who supervises all the money in the world?' I then moved on to anti-royalist sentiments that confused Mum. She revered the monarchy and we sang God Save the Queen at every function, local, church or school. I remember telling her God was not in favour of the monarchical system and reading a text from the Bible that said God gave in to the Israelites and let them have a King like the heathens so they would learn what a ridiculous idea the whole royalty gig was. She was appalled. The only thing worse than a smart arse is one with God on their side.

Mum was ever inventive with her schemes. I decided that it was time to get on board completely and see the next scheme through to its inevitable failure. So, when she approached me with the newspaper and pointed to an ad for paper and junk mail delivery I pulled out all the stops. If she was shocked at my apparent enthusiasm, she didn't say a word. She was elated.

Mum bought a notebook. She phoned the woman. We picked up our papers, and were given a territory. We folded the papers and set off. 'Crikey,' said Mum when we arrived at a hilly area 45 minutes from home. 'Oh, well, I guess we have to prove ourselves and get a better area later.'

I said nothing. Any success I might have ending these Get Rich Slow Schemes depended on my keeping my mouth shut and letting Mum work it out for herself.

We sat in the car and worked out how to cover the territory, poring over the street directory. I drove, did my bit of letterboxing and then met her. This was going very well.

Mum was triumphant.

After four hours we finished the territory, and I was sitting quietly in the car waiting for her to arrive when I looked in the rear vision mirror. Mum appeared over the top of the hill. My mouth dropped open. She was running down the hill, sprinting towards some invisible finish line. I had never seen my mother run. However, it was soon apparent why – a huge, loping German Shepherd was on her heels, barking and snapping. I backed the car, reached over and opened the door. Mum leapt into the car, wheezing like there was no tomorrow. The dog pawed at the window. Mum poked her tongue out at it. I'd never seen her do THAT either.

'That's one cranky animal. We'll avoid that house in future,' I said.

Mum blushed. 'It wasn't at a house. I ... er...'

'What the...?'

'Well,' said Mum. 'I had to go. You know. Brisk walking does that...'

'Oh,' I said as light dawned.

'Number...'

'Yes.'

'How did you wipe...'

'With my undies.'

'Oh my, that's why you're hanging on to your dress.'

'Yes,' she said.

We laughed uncontrollably. We laughed 'til we cried. We couldn't stop. I couldn't shake the image of my mother hiding in the bush, burying her undies and being found by a dog who gave chase. Every time we drew breath and thought we had our mirth under control, we started again.

'Let's just go home, Mum.'

'On no,' she said. 'I never leave a job unfinished.'

'You just proved that,' I said, as we fell about laughing again.

Mum insisted we take the papers back to the women. We both got out. We still couldn't stop laughing. It was a windy day and Mum fought to hold her dress 'I'm going to carry spare nickers after this,' she said. I was of the opinion we presented a ridiculous pair and should throw the handful of papers in the bin back home, but Mum wouldn't hear of it. We leaned on the supervisor's rendered brick fence for many minutes still unable to compose ourselves. When I declared I was leaving, Mum pulled herself up straight, grabbed her dress tightly and with head held high marched down the path.

I waited in the car. Mum came back and got out her notebook. Her calculations didn't take long – she was a Maths Whizz.

'What did we make?' I asked.

'Well, if we take out petrol ... 50 cents each.'

You're useless!

My first job was at a roadside vegetable stall. I was twelve. I rode there on my bike, weighed fruit and vegetables and was shouted at by the crabby woman who grew the vegetables. I once got the price wrong and had two bob taken out of my pay. My mother was a grocery store manager, but it was quite obvious I had inherited none of her talent.

After high school, and before nurse training at the San, I worked at the SHF. The place was never the same after that. Not only was I slow off the mark, I wrecked things. I started in some steamy room packing Vegelinks into tins. I could never fit the right number in and no matter how I tried the last one was always torn and squished and had to be thrown out. After a few days of this malarkey I was thrown out, although they were kind enough to call it a 'transfer'. I was put on the Weet-Bix machine. As the women deftly picked up 6 in each hand and place them precisely in the boxes, I picked six up in each hand and broke the outside ones - four broken out of twelve was not considered acceptable.

I was moved to the cornflakes line. There were twelve women, six to a line. They were not impressed with inexperienced staff fresh from school, so they gave no advice or assistance but sat there scowling or gossiping about their sex lives - all this with a beady eye on me, waiting to giggle at my discomfort. I pretended to be deaf, which didn't bother them much when they were yakking, but annoyed the hell out of them when they wanted to tell me what to do.

Six jobs per side, 1. Catch the cornflakes out of the shute into a plastic bag and place on conveyer belt, 2. & 3. Are a little hazy - I probably never caught on anyway, 4. Someone rolled down the plastic bag. 5. Someone put the toy in. 6. Goodness only knows. I managed the toy insertion quite well, but it was on the Catch the Cornflakes that I really stuffed up. I only managed to catch 2 out of 3 on a good day. I didn't have many good days. When you missed the cornflakes they landed in a bin at your feet. With my imprecise muddling this had to be taken away often, which meant both lines shut down.

Now while the women showed no interest in efficiency and speed to deliver more than necessary they were appalled at my ineptness. I told the foreman I couldn't keep up with the machine and he sped it up. Greaaat! Now I was catching one in four. I had watched how he sped the machine up a few times and when he was gone I opened the hatch and slowed it down. The women gasped, but I caught every single one then. However, the machine, and thus all 12 women were forced to speeds a snail would be ashamed of. They murmured and complained in suitable Biblical fashion so I hummed a very slow waltz. Out of tune. The foreman would return and speed it up. I would slow it down. It broke. They sent an electrician. My brother.

'It was you, wasn't it Sis,' he declared as he set about fixing the machine. It took half an hour. I pretended to have a power nap.

As soon as he left I started again. The foreman was suspicious, but for some strange reason none of the women told him. He looked at me through narrowed eyes when the thing shut down the second time.

'He'll go and tell the big bosses,' warned the women.

'Rubbish,' I said, 'you don't really think he's going to go over to the office and say a teenager worked out how to do his job?'

I was transferred to a far corner of the factory where all that was required of me was to pick the skins off peanuts as they went along a conveyer belt. The peanuts had already been tumbled so there wasn't much skin left. It was here that I discovered an unusual phenomenon. Much like sitting a train the train next to you is moving, it was hard to tell just what was moving and what wasn't.

A friend came and watched me. I was mesmerised. 'Hey, Brooks, you're not getting many skins there. Those peanuts are rushing past and you're missing them.'

'Oh,' I said, 'the peanuts aren't moving – the machine is. If you watch it long enough that's what happens.'

She laughed and walked off. However, my school nemesis was on the prowl, she'd been working there two years and full of self-importance. My ineptitude was her opportunity.

'Jeez, Brooks. Not the dux of the school here are ya? You're completely useless.'

'I know,' I said, 'isn't it marvellous. I'm getting the same pay as you and I'm absolutely rubbish at everything.

The love of a mother

She is just another confused traveller in the winding journey of life, this mother of mine. Trying to work it out as she goes along. Doing her damnedest to keep life on solid ground. She has watched me flying into life changing the rules, changing everything. How frightening that must have been for her added to the tragedies I collected like stamps, this exuberant, ethereal spirit that was her child. She must be tired of life's disasters. Tired of my disasters. Weary of my crusades. From her world of straight lines and square boxes I must look like an uncontrollable force of nature, unpredictable, terrifying. She was relentless in her pursuit of fairness and a hard day's work. She enjoyed the concrete side of motherhood; she would tick off 'clean, warm, tummies full, tucked up safe in bed', and then she would rest.

She loves me and wanted to pay me the ultimate compliment in life by making me like her, the only way to be in this world that is far from heaven and full of mystery and questions. She does not like the questions; she calls them tests of faith, and brings out the answers given to her by her own mother and buries the subject. This is how she must live. And she sits and watches me, I who question everything, and wants to lie down. Nothing exhausts her like stray emotions and the twists and turns of the mind. It is all a waste of time. I remember as a child her telling the neighbours, 'She wears me out just listening to her, that child'. She would like to rein me in. How I chafed at those obligatory parting parental words of, 'Be careful'. And now that I am a parent those are the very words that are on my lips, the benediction of be careful, be safe, come home again, back to me because no matter how angry I am with you or how little I understand you, you are mine and without you in my life, I am undone. I know all that now when I hear those words.

I went to her and asked if she would like to do some ordinary thing. She loves to soak her feet and I suggested she buy a foot spa. It was an olive branch and we have needed many olive branches since my arrival in her life. She waited patiently while I visited the doctor. We had lunch. When I took her home she said, 'I'm sorry for ever hurting you.'

'It's Ok, mum.'

Mother's Day – Unsentimentally yours,...

I looked in the saucepan cupboard today and saw you, Mum, even though you've been dead for nearly a decade. No, you weren't haunting me. You'd have no truck with that kind of supernatural nonsense. It was a reflection of me, head dangling upside down, looking for some utensil or other. Yes, I'm more like you as I grow older - 'You poor thing,' I hear you say, 'fancy looking like me'.

I haven't put flowers on your grave. I find no particular nostalgia in cemeteries. I know that would disappoint you a bit. I remember taking you and Auntie Gwen for the Mother's Day Meander. You and Auntie Gwen would make little bouquets - at least Auntie Gwen did, you weren't much chop with flower arranging. Baby's breath and bracken fern, and a white Chrysanthemum.

The two of you got lost every year as I dragged reluctant feet behind, muttering that I would never be as daft as either of you - making promises to aged aunts on deathbeds to memorialise them every blooming Mother's Day. I'd sit on a headstone (Linda don't do that!) while the two of you wandered until one would cry out - 'I found Aunt Dolly!', or 'here's Cousin George!' and I'd think, if the relatives were that dashed important how did you manage to lose them every year? It wasn't as if they'd gone on holiday or moved anywhere. Then you'd chat to each other, which was kind of nice, seeing you so rarely saw eye to eye other times. And the memories would flow. Then you'd glance at your watches, look around for me, perhaps surprised that I was easier to find than the dead, and I'd sigh with relief and take you both home, making sure that neither of you expected me to keep up that tradition.

You went rain or shine, until you were weak and stumbling, coughing and weaving, lumping sleek walking frames on sodden ground, keeping ancient promises to cold earth. You were angry that last time when I wouldn't take you. You had bronchitis. We had a tense battle, while you gave me that sharp eagle eye and tight-lipped silence I knew so well. You were thinking, as soon as she leaves I'll go myself if it kills me. So I went to the car, brought a Chrysanthemum to you and sat down. When you saw I was staying you cried, then I cried and we held each other as I muttered about honouring the living, especially those on the verge of pneumonia and hospital, who should listen to daughters who know better.

If a girl's father is the first man she falls in love with then perhaps a girl's mother is the first person she wages war with, cuts the eye teeth of independence on, wrestles for the loosening of the apron strings. From you I learned there was no cause or social justice that wasn't worth fighting for, there was no truth too rough to speak, no front door to the house of family so tightly shut that you can't knock and enter, no matter how bitter the argument or how terse the last words on the lips. No forgiveness that would be withheld, no pride too great to say, or hear 'I'm sorry. I was wrong.'

Author

Linda Brooks lives in Adelaide. She writes nonfiction, poetry, fiction and short stories. She has published and illustrated children's books. She has a BA Hons in Creative Writing from Southern Cross University. She gained a publisher for her childhood memoir *A Curious & Inelegant Childhood*. She has written a nonfiction book on living with Asperger's Syndrome *I'm not broken, I'm just different* and the children's book *Callan the Chameleon* with contributions from Professor Tony Attwood.

Published in anthologies: 'Coastlines' 5, 6, 7 & 8 by Southern Cross University; 'Wood, Bricks & Stone'; 'Grieve', 'Third Wednesday Poets' and 'Longing for Solitude'. Awards: Rebecca Coyle Scholarship for Hons; first prize for The Legacy University Level Creative Writing Award; first prize in the Gabe Reynaud Creative Writing Award and the Mater Misericordiae Grieve Writing Award.

A registered nurse and advocate for disability in a previous life, Linda has a rich background in listening to the stories of others, never shying away from the darker, gritty tales. And yet, humour is never far away. Linda enjoys hearing from her readers (even if they've found typos):

lindaruthbrooks@bigpond.com

Nonfiction:
I'm not broken, I'm just different
(on Asperger's with Professor Tony Attwood)
A Curious and Inelegant Childhood

Verse novel:
The day the war ended

Adult fiction:
Behind Whispering Hands
The Unprize
A broken hallelujah
Scarlett doesn't live here anymore
Under the Bracken Fern

Children's books:
A Tabby Never Forgets
Callan the Chameleon (Asperger's Syndrome)
Dusty Bunny's Very Important Job
Izzy & Pudding the Cat
I want a monkey!
Madam Iris Bigglesworth
The Banyula Tales - 6 stories
Who Stole Christmas?

Publisher of the anthologies:
We are Australian'
The Great Australian Shed
Waltzing Matilda